Excel

Get the Results You Wa...

Year 6
Thinking Skills
Tests

**Sharon Dalgleish,
Tanya Dalgleish
& Hamish McLean**

PASCAL
PRESS

Completely new edition incorporating late 2020 Selective School changes

ISBN 978 1 74125 703 8

Pascal Press Pty Ltd
PO Box 250
Glebe NSW 2037
(02) 9198 1748
www.pascalpress.com.au

Publisher: Vivienne Joannou
Project editor: Mark Dixon
Edited by Mark Dixon and Rosemary Peers
Answers checked by Dale Little and Melinda Amaral
Cover by DiZign Pty Ltd
Typeset by Grizzly Graphics (Leanne Richters)
Printed by Vivar Printing/Green Giant Press

Contents

INTRODUCTION

ABOUT THIS BOOK

This book has been written to help develop students' thinking skills. Thinking skills involve two disciplines: critical thinking and problem solving.

Critical thinking means the ability to analyse a claim or argument; identify whether it is flawed or uses correct reasoning; and determine whether the evidence, assumptions and conclusion are warranted.

Problem solving as a thinking skill means the ability to use numerical or mathematical skills to work out solutions to problems. These include visualising and rotating solids in three-dimensional space; ordering a number of objects based on comparisons and characteristics; analysing graphs and diagrams; and solving mathematical puzzles involving numbers, shapes and time.

Critical-thinking and problem-solving skills are valuable in everyday life as well as in many fields of endeavour students might eventually embark upon.

The first section of this book teaches students 20 thinking skills. Each thinking skill is first defined, then a sample question is provided and the solution is worked through for the student as a teaching/learning exercise. Then two practice questions are provided. These are for the student to attempt independently. The solutions are worked through in the answer section of the book.

This section is followed by eight practice tests comprising 20 questions each. Each test includes an equal mixture of critical-thinking and problem-solving questions.

Answers and detailed explanations are provided at the back of the book. Most answers include the working out.

If you would like to use this book to help you prepare specifically for the Selective High School Test, you can merge two Sample Tests and have your child complete the two tests in 40 minutes.

One test will therefore comprise 40 questions, which is equivalent to the length of the Thinking Skills paper in the NSW Selective High School Placement Test. For example, you could merge Sample Test 1A with Sample Test 1B to form Test 1.

ABOUT THE SELECTIVE HIGH SCHOOL TEST

The NSW Selective High School Placement Test consists of four sections:

- **Reading** (30 questions in 40 minutes)
- **Thinking Skills** (40 questions in 40 minutes)
- **Mathematical Reasoning** (35 questions in 40 minutes)
- **Writing** (one question in 30 minutes).

The tests, except Writing, are in multiple-choice form, with each question being of equal value. Marks are awarded for each correct answer and applicants are advised to guess the answer if they are uncertain.

HOW THE RESULTS ARE USED BY PUBLIC SCHOOLS

Entry to selective high schools is based on academic merit. In 2022 changes were made to the allocation of places. Under the Equity Placement Model, up to 20% of places are held for members of the following disadvantaged and under-represented groups:

- students from low socio-educational advantage backgrounds
- First Nations students
- rural and remote students
- students with disability.

It is important to remember that the places allocated under the Equity Placement Model will not necessarily be filled. In 2023, the first year of this new system, less than 10% of these places were offered. This means that more than 90% of the places were offered to general applicants. The new system has helped close the educational gap in participation from disadvantaged groups without having a significant impact on other applicants.

Students no longer receive a test score or placement rank. The new performance report will instead place students in one of the following categories:

- top 10% of candidates
- next 15% of candidates
- next 25% of candidates
- lowest 50% of candidates.

This change addresses privacy and wellbeing concerns including unhealthy competition between students. The sole purpose of the test is to identify students who would benefit from the chance to study at a selective school and, since it doesn't test knowledge of the curriculum, there is no diagnostic merit in the test—unlike the NAPLAN test, which can help identify areas where children can improve.

Minimum entry scores for selective schools are no longer published because these change from year to year and depend on the number of applicants, their relative performance and the number of families who decline an offer. Students placed on the reserve list no longer receive a numerical rank; instead an indication of how long it will take to receive an offer, based on previous years, is provided.

A selection committee for each selective high school decides which students are to be offered places. These committees also decide how many students are to be placed on the reserve list. Should a student with a confirmed offer turn down a place at a selective school, the place will be offered to the first student on the reserve list.

There is an appeals panel for illness or other mitigating circumstances. All applicants are advised of the outcome. The NSW Government provides detailed information on the application and selection process for parents on the Selective High School Placement Test. This is available from: https://education.nsw.gov.au/parents-and-carers/learning/tests-and-exams/selective-school-test.

Sample test papers are also available on this website.

ADVICE TO STUDENTS

Each question in the NSW Selective High School Placement Test is multiple choice. This means you have to choose the correct answer from the given options. You need to read the question in the test booklet then mark your answer on a separate answer sheet.

We have included a sample answer sheet in this book—similar to those you will be given in the actual test—for you to practise on.

Under time pressure and test conditions it is possible to miss a question and leave a line on the answer sheet blank. Always check that your answer on the separate answer sheet is written down next to the right number. For instance, check that your answer to question 15 is written down against the number 15 on the answer sheet. There is nothing worse than finding out you have missed a space, especially when time is running short.

Some of the more challenging Thinking Skills problem-solving questions, for example, could take you up to 10 minutes to complete to begin with, as you may use diagrams or tables to help you solve them. Remember that the more questions you do of this same type, the faster you will become—until you know exactly how to solve them.

Thinking Skills sample answer sheet

Mark your answers here.

To answer each question, fill in the appropriate circle for your chosen answer.

Use a pencil. If you make a mistake or change your mind, erase and try again.

You can make extra copies of this answer sheet to mark your answers to all the Sample Tests in this book.

Test A

	A B C D		A B C D		A B C D		A B C D
1	O O O O	6	O O O O	11	O O O O	16	O O O O
2	A B C D O O O O	7	A B C D O O O O	12	A B C D O O O O	17	A B C D O O O O
3	A B C D O O O O	8	A B C D O O O O	13	A B C D O O O O	18	A B C D O O O O
4	A B C D O O O O	9	A B C D O O O O	14	A B C D O O O O	19	A B C D O O O O
5	A B C D O O O O	10	A B C D O O O O	15	A B C D O O O O	20	A B C D O O O O

Test B

	A B C D		A B C D		A B C D		A B C D
1	O O O O	6	O O O O	11	O O O O	16	O O O O
2	A B C D O O O O	7	A B C D O O O O	12	A B C D O O O O	17	A B C D O O O O
3	A B C D O O O O	8	A B C D O O O O	13	A B C D O O O O	18	A B C D O O O O
4	A B C D O O O O	9	A B C D O O O O	14	A B C D O O O O	19	A B C D O O O O
5	A B C D O O O O	10	A B C D O O O O	15	A B C D O O O O	20	A B C D O O O O

Identifying the main idea

- The main idea is the idea or conclusion the creator of the text wants you to accept is true. It's often stated at the beginning of a text but it could be at the end or anywhere else in the text. The rest of the text will support or add to that main idea, or give you reason to believe it.
- Read the question carefully and think about what the creator of the text wants you to accept. Underline the sentence that you think could be the main idea. Check to see if the rest of the text gives you reasons to believe this main idea. Read each answer option in turn to evaluate if it expresses the main idea. Quickly eliminate any answers that are definitely wrong. Decide which of the statements best expresses the main idea you found.

SAMPLE QUESTION

Peaceful Valley Cemetery is one of the oldest cemeteries in our region and is a place steeped in history. It is the final resting place of many well-known Peaceful Valley locals. But Peaceful Valley Council needs your help to uncover some missing links that will help piece together some unsolved mysteries. Council is trying to source personal histories of all those currently buried in the cemetery. Our Council volunteer history team is keen to hear from any relatives or locals with information. Please phone the team on Council's general number or email any information to localhistory@peacefulvalleycouncil.

Which statement best expresses the main idea of the text?

A Peaceful Valley Cemetery is one of the oldest in the region and steeped in history.

B Council wants to source personal histories of people buried in the cemetery.

C Peaceful Valley Cemetery dates back to the 1870s and contains over 5000 graves.

D There are missing links and unsolved mysteries in the cemetery.

B is correct. The main idea that the creator of the text wants you to accept is that Council wants to source personal histories of people buried in the cemetery. The rest of the text supports this main idea by giving information about why Council wants the information and how people can help to supply it.

A is incorrect. This background information is used in the introduction but it is not the main idea the creator of the texts wants you to accept.

C is incorrect. This information is not in the text so it cannot be the main idea.

D is incorrect. This is a reason to believe the main idea; it supports the main idea.

Practice questions

1 When surging floodwaters began to engulf a property in flood-stricken northern Riverglen last week, two young wombats were in desperate strife. One was splashing as it was frantically swimming trying to reach a fence. The other was clinging to the wire fence and trying to keep its head above water. Luckily the property owner saw them and was able to safely rescue both distressed animals. She called the local wildlife rescue organisation for help and the wombats are now with a wildlife carer. Once they have recovered, the carer will ensure they have all the skills they'll need for an eventual release back into the wild.

Which statement best expresses the main idea of the text?

A A woman saw the two distressed wombats in water on her property.

B Wombats are good swimmers, using a stroke similar to dog paddle.

C The rescued wombats will eventually be released back into the wild.

D Two wombats were rescued in floodwaters in northern Riverglen.

☞ Answers and explanations on page 72

Identifying the main idea

2 Putting your houseplants outside when it rains can be just the tonic they need. There are so many benefits of rainwater for houseplants. Tap water holds salts that can build up in the soil and stop your plant from growing. Rainwater can help to flush away this build-up. Rainwater also has more oxygen than tap water. Higher levels of oxygen can prevent root rot. Plus rainwater is higher in nitrogen. Nitrogen keeps plants looking lush and green. Just don't leave your delicate houseplants out in a storm!

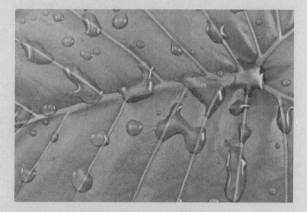

Which statement best expresses the main idea of the text?

A Don't leave houseplants outside in a storm.

B Most fertilisers use chemically derived nitrogen to turn leaves green.

C Putting houseplants outside when it rains can be good for them.

D Rainwater has many benefits for indoor houseplants.

☞ Answers and explanations on page 72

Identifying a conclusion that must be true

- To draw a conclusion you need to read and assess all the information and evidence provided. A conclusion can only be true if it is supported by evidence. A potential conclusion can be eliminated if there is evidence that contradicts it or if there is no evidence or only incomplete evidence to support it.
- Read the question carefully. Judge which conclusion must be true based on the evidence in the text. As you read the answer options, try to quickly eliminate any potential conclusion that has evidence to contradict it. Also eliminate any conclusion that is neither proved nor disproved because the evidence is incomplete or unavailable.

SAMPLE QUESTION

Conrad has Chess Club on Tuesdays and Fridays. When he got home from Chess Club he noticed the owner of unit 1 unlocking the gate to the barbecue area behind their block of units.

The groundskeeper opens the barbecue area and checks the gas bottle to see if it needs replacing every day except Friday and Saturday when the unit 4 owner opens the barbecue area and checks the gas bottle. Apart from the groundskeeper, the unit 1 owner is the only other person allowed to replace the gas bottle. If the unit 4 owner notices the gas bottle needs replacing, she gives the barbecue area key to the unit 1 owner.

Based on the above information, which one of the following must be true?

A Today is Sunday and the gas bottle needs replacing.

B Today is Monday and the unit 4 owner will replace the barbecue gas bottle.

C Today is Friday and the gas bottle needs replacing.

D The groundskeeper is at work today and the gas bottle does not need replacing.

To answer this question, you need to use the information provided to draw your own conclusion and to rule out the options which cannot be true.

C is correct. From the information given, the only time the unit 1 owner has the key to unlock the barbecue area is when the groundskeeper is not at work and the gas bottle needs to be replaced. The groundskeeper does not work on Fridays and Saturdays. Conrad noticed the unit 1 owner when he got home from Chess Club. He has Chess Club on Tuesdays and Fridays so today must be Friday.

A is incorrect. It cannot be Sunday because Conrad has been to Chess Club.

B is incorrect. It cannot be Monday because Conrad has been to Chess Club.

D is incorrect. It cannot be a day when the groundskeeper is working because the unit 1 owner would not be opening the gate to the barbecue area.

🔧 Practice questions

1 Yuki's school was selecting students for a series of drama workshops. A well-respected actor-director had volunteered her time as drama mentor to work with the school on the workshops. As well as considering students' playwriting ability, the school and the mentor interviewed students individually and also gave them a drama improvisation challenge. If a student had proof of existing theatrical experience, then they only had to pass the interview. If they had limited theatrical experience, then they had to do exceptionally well in the interview as well as in the drama improvisation challenge.

Based on the above information, which one of the following must be true?

A Yuki has no theatrical experience but passed the interview and the drama improvisation challenge and was selected for the workshops.

B Yuki did not do well in the drama improvisation challenge and has very little limited theatrical experience but passed the interview and was selected for the workshops.

Identifying a conclusion that must be true

C Yuki passed the interview but did badly in the drama improvisation challenge so was not selected for the workshops.

D Yuki only just passed the interview but has proof of extensive theatrical experience and did exceptionally well in the drama improvisation challenge so was selected for the workshops.

2 A human circus, 'Tumble Bees', is keeping track of the skill sets of its four most talented performers: Hana, Riku, Adele and Robbie. The company has worked out that if a performer is good on the high wire, they are also good on the trapeze. If a performer is good at trapeze, they are also good at gymnastics. No performer who is good at trapeze is also good at juggling.

Based on the above information, which one of the following must be true?

A If Hana is good at juggling, she is also good on the highwire.

B If Riku is not good at juggling, he is also not good on the trapeze.

C If Adele is not good on the high wire, she is also not good on the trapeze.

D If Robbie is a good juggler, he won't be good on the high wire.

Identifying a conclusion that is not possible

- Before drawing a conclusion you need to consider all the evidence. For a conclusion to be true it should be supported by evidence. You can work out when a conclusion is not possible because there won't be evidence to support it.
- Read the question carefully. When working out your answer you should try to quickly eliminate any options that are obviously incorrect. In this type of question these will be the conclusions that are possible. This will narrow down your choice. Judge which conclusion cannot be true by deciding which one has no evidence to support it.

SAMPLE QUESTION

If we don't all pass the test this Friday, then Mr Cross will cancel the end-of-term class party.

If we have the party and it is successful, then we might be able to convince Mr Cross to let us have another party next term. But it won't be a success if the whole class doesn't work as a team to plan the party and to clean up afterwards. And if the party is not successful, then it will be the last party Mr Cross will let us have!

If the above statements are correct, which one of the following is not possible?

A The party did not go ahead even though the whole class worked as a team to plan it.

B The party was cancelled even though everyone passed the test on Friday.

C The class did not work as a team to clean up after the party but Mr Cross let them have a party in term two.

D The class worked as a team to plan the party and clean up afterwards but the party was not a success.

C is correct. From the information given you can draw the conclusion that if the class does not work as a team to clean up after the party, then it will not be a success. If it is not a success, then Mr Cross will not let them have any more parties. So this conclusion cannot be true.

A is incorrect. This statement could be true if not all the students passed the test on Friday.

B is incorrect. This statement could be true. Just because the text says the party will be cancelled if they don't all pass the test, it does not mean there cannot be another reason why the test might be cancelled even if they all pass it.

D is incorrect. This statement could be true. The information tells us that the party will not be a success if these conditions are not met. However, meeting these conditions does not guarantee that the party will be a success.

Practice questions

1 Five friends took the same Maths test with 20 questions. The results recorded both accuracy and speed in completing the test. The friends compared their results.

- Rose was slower than Ilja but Ilja was slower than Bree.
- Bree was faster than Josh but got three questions wrong.
- Yifan answered all the questions correctly but took the longest.
- Josh answered more questions correctly than Ilja but finished after him.
- Ilja finished second but got two questions wrong.

If the above information is true, which one of the sentences below cannot be true?

A Josh got more answers wrong than Yifan.

B Bree was not the first to finish the test.

C Bree was faster than Rose.

D Bree got the least answers correct.

Identifying a conclusion that is not possible

2 **Luca:** 'Let's go to the beach on Saturday.'

Sofia: 'I can't. I have to go shopping for a birthday present for my dad. If I don't go on Saturday, I probably won't get another chance.'

Luca: 'If you don't get him a present, your dad will be in a bad mood!'

Sofia: 'Yes! But if he's in a good mood, I'm hoping he might let me go to Violet's weekend camping party next month. If he's in a bad mood, there's no way he will let me.'

Based on the above information, which one of the following **cannot** be true?

A   Sofia didn't go shopping on Saturday but her dad said yes to the camping party.

B   Sofia's dad was in a good mood but he didn't let her go to the camping party.

C   Sofia went shopping on Saturday and bought the present but her dad didn't let her go to the camping party.

D   Sofia's dad was in a bad mood but he let her go to the weekend camping party.

☞ Answers and explanations on pages 72–73

Identifying evidence that leads to a conclusion

- To draw a conclusion you need supporting data or evidence. Sometimes you can't work out a conclusion because there isn't enough evidence available.
- These types of questions ask you to identify which information allows you to know a conclusion or result. These questions are not asking you to draw a conclusion but instead to judge which option(s) help you know what the conclusion is. You need to eliminate the options that don't lead to a conclusion or that don't help you work out a conclusion.

SAMPLE QUESTION

Tamika's class had to agree on a theme for the mural they were to paint on the external wall of the assembly hall. They decided to hold a vote and narrowed the choices down to three: a rainforest, the school's history or a tribute to their community's First Nations people.

Everyone in the class had two votes but could not vote for the same option twice. The teacher said they would only use an option if everyone in the class voted for it. If this didn't happen, they would choose a different way to decide the mural's theme. Every theme got at least one vote.

Which statement below allows you to know the result of the vote?

A Every student voted for either the school's history or a tribute to their community's First Nations people, or both.

B The rainforest was the most popular vote.

C No student voted for both the school's history and the rainforest.

D Only two students voted for the school's history.

To answer this question you need to judge which option helps you know the result. Note that you are not being asked to work out the result.

C is correct. Since everyone had to vote for two of the three themes, knowing that no student voted for both the school's history and the rainforest tells you that everyone must have voted for the tribute to their community's First Nations people. Also the tribute to their community's First Nations people must be the theme that everyone voted for because every

theme got at least one vote. The outcome will therefore be to paint a tribute to the community's First Nations people.

Practice questions

1 At the end of each week Mr Seric gives students mini tests in punctuation, grammar and spelling. Each test is marked out of 10 for a total possible score of 30 marks.

Last week Nandi and Marco achieved the same mark in grammar and the same overall mark of 24 out of 30 but different marks in spelling and punctuation.

Which statement below helps you work out Marco's result in spelling?

A Nandi and Marco achieved the same result in grammar of 9 out of 10 but received different marks for punctuation and spelling.

B Marco achieved 9 out of 10 in grammar and did better than Nandi in spelling but did not do as well as Nandi in punctuation.

C Marco achieved 9 out of 10 in grammar while Nandi scored 7 out of 10 in spelling and 8 out of 10 in punctuation.

D Marco and Nandi achieved different results in punctuation and spelling.

2 Husain's class decided to buy a gift for their music teacher. They could buy a music store gift voucher, two concert tickets or a book about one of the teacher's favourite bands. They decided to have a vote as the fairest way to choose a gift. Each student in the class got two votes and they had to vote for two different gifts. The class decided they should only accept one of the gifts if everyone voted for it. If this did not happen, they would vote again on a different selection of gifts. Every gift received at least one vote.

Which statement below provides the evidence that allows you to work out the result of the vote?

A Everyone voted for either the concert tickets or the book, or both.

B The music store gift voucher was the most popular choice.

C Only two people voted for the concert tickets.

D No-one voted for both the concert tickets and the music store gift voucher.

Identifying an assumption

- An assumption is not stated in a text. It is something missing that has been assumed or taken for granted to draw a conclusion. An assumption is not necessarily true but the person making the assumption believes it is. For this reason, making assumptions can lead to incorrect conclusions!

- To identify an assumption in a text, read the text carefully and identify the conclusion that has been made. Next identify the evidence or reasoning on which that conclusion is based. Finally read and think about each assumption answer option listed. Which one of those options would you need to take for granted in order to draw that conclusion from the evidence or reasoning?

- You can think about it like this:

EVIDENCE + ASSUMPTION = CONCLUSION. In order to answer the question, you need to find the missing assumption to complete the equation.

SAMPLE QUESTION

Ella runs into her friend Oscar after school. Oscar is carrying a guitar.

Ella: 'I was going to ask if you wanted to come for a swim. But I see you are on your way to a guitar lesson.'

Oscar: 'No, I'm just dropping off the guitar for my sister. Let's go for a swim!'

Which assumption has Ella made in order to draw her conclusion?

A Oscar is carrying a guitar after school.

B Anyone carrying a guitar after school must be on their way to a guitar lesson.

C Oscar is dropping off the guitar for his sister.

D Oscar is on the way to a guitar lesson.

B is correct. For Ella's conclusion to hold, it has to be assumed that anyone carrying a guitar after school must be on their way to a lesson: Oscar is carrying a guitar after school + anyone carrying a guitar after school must be on the way to a lesson means therefore Oscar is on his way to a guitar lesson.

A is incorrect. This is the evidence or reason that Ella has used to draw her conclusion.

C is incorrect. This is the real reason why Oscar is carrying the guitar, not the assumption that Ella has made.

D is incorrect. This is Ella's conclusion, not the missing assumption.

 Practice questions

1   Willow and Zac borrowed Willow's brother's car to drive to the store.

Willow: 'If we scratch the car, my brother will be really angry.'

Zac: 'Be careful then. We must not scratch the car!'

Which assumption has Zac made in order to draw his conclusion?

A Willow does not have a car of her own.

B Willow and Zac must not scratch the car.

C Willow and Zac must not do anything to make Willow's brother angry.

D If Willow and Zac scratch the car, Willow's brother will be angry.

2 The local council announced it would install concrete median islands along the main beachfront road to slow down the traffic.

Mr Lees wrote an email to the council: 'If concrete median islands are installed, they will damage cars reversing from beachfront parking bays. Therefore they must not be installed.'

Which assumption has Mr Lees made in order to draw his conclusion?

A We should not do something that will cause damage to cars.

B The concrete median islands should not be installed.

C If concrete median islands are installed, they will damage reversing cars.

D The beachfront is a busy area for cars and pedestrians.

Identifying correct reasoning

- When someone presents a point of view or makes a claim or an argument, they use reasoning to support that point of view or argument. Their reasoning must make sense and be based on the facts available.
- When presented with a claim or argument, you need to decide what it is that the speaker or writer wants you to accept as true. Then you need to analyse their reasoning. If you accept that their reasoning is correct, you might accept their argument. If the reasoning does not make sense or is flawed, you can reject the claim or argument.
- These kinds of questions ask you to judge if the reasoning is correct. Read the question carefully. When working out your answer, quickly eliminate answers that are obviously incorrect until you find the answer that is correct.

SAMPLE QUESTION

The skills required to use a stand-up paddleboard and to surf are similar.
- Anyone who can use a stand-up paddleboard can also surf.
- Anyone who can use a stand-up paddleboard can also ski.
- Not everyone who can surf can also use a stand-up paddleboard.
- Anyone who can surf and ski can also use a stand-up paddleboard.

Willow: Reba has been skiing for a few years. She will have no trouble surfing.
Hunter: Dexter is unable to use a stand-up paddleboard so he won't be able to surf.

If the information in the box is true, whose reasoning is correct?

A Willow only

B Hunter only

C Both Willow and Hunter

D Neither Willow not Hunter

To answer this question you need to judge if the reasoning used to draw the conclusion is correct. If the reasoning is not correct or is flawed, then the conclusion drawn cannot be relied upon as true.

A is correct. The information in the box says that anyone who can surf can also use a stand-up paddleboard and anyone who can use a stand-up paddleboard can also surf so Willow is correct in reasoning that if Reba can surf, she will also be able to ski but not everyone who can surf can use a stand-up paddleboard.

B is incorrect. The information in the box does not say that if you can't use a stand-up paddleboard, you won't be able to surf either. It only says that not everyone who can surf can use a stand-up paddleboard.

C and D are incorrect by a process of elimination.

⚙ Practice questions

1 Everyone on the soccer team gets to vote for the end-of-season party food. They can vote for pizzas, burgers, sushi or fish and chips. Everyone has one vote. There are two teams of 11 players, two reserves and a coach.

Alice: Whatever gets 13 votes will be the winner.

Ned: If a food gets 7 votes, it could be the winner.

If the information in the box is true, whose reasoning is correct?

A Alice only

B Ned only

C Both Alice and Ned

D Neither Alice nor Ned

2 There are four steps for an animal to learn a behaviour from another animal:

- It must watch the other animal.
- It must remember what it saw the animal do.
- It must have the ability to perform that behaviour itself.
- It must be motivated to perform that behaviour, such as by a reward like access to food.

Lana: Rats can learn behaviour from other rats. When a rat is placed in a box where there's a button that if stepped on releases a food pellet into the box, the rat eventually learns that it can press the bar to release food whenever it wants.

Eddie: Crows learn behaviour from other crows. Crows have been observed working in groups. One crow props open the lid of a garbage bin to allow other crows access to food scraps within. Then the crows switch places and a different crow props open the lid so they all have a chance to eat.

Diana: Quolls can learn from other quolls. Scientists are training northern quolls not to attack cane toads which are poisonous for them. Scientists have been feeding the quolls small dead toads laced with cane toad toxin so that they vomit and learn to avoid cane toads in future. This learned behaviour should help quolls survive cane-toad infestation.

If the above information is true, whose reasoning is correct?

A   Lana only

B   Eddie only

C   Diana only

D   Lana and Diana only

Identifying flawed reasoning

- When someone presents a point of view or makes a claim or an argument, they use reasoning to support that point of view or argument. Their reasoning must make sense and be based on the facts available.
- When you read or listen to a point of view or argument you need to analyse the reasoning. If the reasoning does not make sense or is flawed, then you can reject the claim or argument.
- Some questions tell you that the reasoning in a claim or argument is flawed. This type of question asks you to identify the flaw or mistake that has been made. Read the question carefully. When working out your answer, quickly eliminate options that are obviously incorrect until you find the answer that is correct: the one that shows the flawed reasoning.

SAMPLE QUESTION

> Meg wants to join a local water-polo team. To qualify, players must be able to swim 20 laps in the pool.

Carter: 'Meg could only swim 15 laps last year. But she has been training all year and can now easily swim 25 laps. So she will definitely be chosen to be in the team this year.'

Which one of the following sentences shows the mistake Carter has made?

A Meg might find that she does not enjoy playing water polo.

B There might not be enough players for a complete water-polo team this year.

C Other sports might also require players to be able to swim 20 laps.

D Swimming laps might not be the only criterion used to select players.

D is correct. We know that, to qualify for the water-polo team, players must be able to swim 20 laps in the pool. However, that might not be the only criterion used to select players and it does not mean that anyone who can swim 20 laps will definitely be chosen for the team. So this sentence shows the flaw in Carter's reasoning that Meg will definitely be chosen to be in the team this year: that is, she might not be chosen.

A is incorrect. This might be the case but it does not show a mistake Carter has made since Meg might still be chosen to be in the team.

B is incorrect. This might be the case but Meg could still be chosen for the team so this does not show a mistake Carter has made.

C is incorrect. This might be the case but it does not show a mistake Carter has made.

Practice questions

1. Xavier's school organised a pet–owner lookalike contest at their annual school fete. Each owner could enter the contest only once and with only one pet. On the day of the fete, the owners and their pets were to parade around the school oval. Judges would then score each pair and award prizes for first, second and third place. There would also be a prize for People's Choice, as voted by the audience.

    Xavier's dad entered the contest with their dog Pongo.

Identifying flawed reasoning

Xavier: 'I know that four pairs of owners and pets will get prizes. I hope Dad and Pongo get one!'

Which one of the following sentences shows the mistake Xavier has made?

A   One owner might win a prize for more than one pet.

B   Some pets might not look like their owners so might be disqualified.

C   The People's Choice prizewinner might also come first, second or third.

D   More than twenty pairs of owners and pets might have entered the contest.

2 Matilda works at the local cinema every weekend. The supervisor at the cinema has promised that any workers who were on cleaning duty on the last roster will definitely not be chosen for cleaning duty on the next roster.

Matilda: 'Cleaning duty is the worst! But I didn't get cleaning on the last roster. So that means I will definitely be chosen for cleaning duty on the next roster.'

Which one of the following sentences shows the mistake Matilda has made?

A   Just because a worker who was on cleaning duty on the last roster will not be chosen for cleaning duty on the next roster, it does not mean that any worker who didn't have cleaning duty on the last roster will definitely be given it on the next roster.

B   Just because a worker was on cleaning duty on the last roster, it does not mean that they will not be chosen for cleaning duty on the next roster.

C   Just because Matilda does not like cleaning duty, it does not mean that she won't be chosen for cleaning duty on the next roster.

D   Just because a worker did not get a chance to work cleaning duty on the last roster, it does not mean that they would not have liked cleaning duty.

Identifying additional evidence that strengthens an argument

- When someone makes a claim or presents an argument, they use evidence to convince others to accept that claim. A claim can be strengthened with further evidence or additional information.
- To identify the statement that best supports or most strengthens a claim or an argument, read the text carefully. Identify the claim being made in the text. Then consider the answer options listed and assess the impact of each one on that claim.
- Look for the option that gives further evidence to support the claim or that most strengthens it. Try to quickly eliminate statements which are definitely incorrect or irrelevant to the argument.

SAMPLE QUESTION

When Sung decided to focus on his career as a competitive cyclist he announced that he would have to give up playing for his local tennis club on Saturdays.

Sung's friend Dami said: 'You don't need to give up tennis on Saturdays to have a career as a professional cyclist. It's important to engage in other sports as recreational activities. Tennis is good for you. You enjoy it and you are good at it. You have lots of friends at the tennis club who you can have fun with and you don't have to take tennis competitions too seriously.'

Which one of these statements, if true, most strengthens Dami's argument?

A Tennis is a sport and any sporting activity will help improve Sung's cycling.

B Sung is worried that he needs to concentrate on his strength and fitness.

C Sung's coach says he is too serious and hard on himself and he needs to relax more.

D Top athletes often compete in more than one sport.

To answer this question, you need to assess the statements to determine which one most strengthens the argument by supporting it or providing additional evidence not already mentioned in the text.

C is correct. First identify the argument: Dami is trying to convince Sung that he can continue to enjoy Saturday tennis while focusing on his career as a cyclist. What additional information will strengthen Dami's argument? The additional evidence that supports Dami's argument is that Sung's coach says Sung is too serious and hard on himself and that he needs to relax more.

A is incorrect. It is likely true that any sporting activity will help improve Sung's cycling performance. However, Dami's argument is not about performance and ability; it is about tennis as a recreational or fun activity so this is not the statement that **most** strengthens Dami's claim.

B is incorrect. The claim that Sung worries that he needs to concentrate on his strength and fitness might be true but it is not a statement that supports Dami's argument.

D is incorrect. This statement might be true but it is not an argument that Dami is making so it does not strengthen her argument.

Practice questions

1. A psychiatrist said: 'Many children these days suffer from overstimulation. Overstimulation is when children experience sensory overload. Sensory overload is very unhealthy. It can lead to angry outbursts and tantrums or serious depression. Some parents think that every minute of a child's day needs to be scheduled with activity and learning but children's lives are now too full and include too much pressure and stress. We need to return to simpler times when children played outdoors after school and had free time to relax and unwind.'

Which one of these statements, if true, most strengthens the psychiatrist's argument?

   A Children's brains are always switched on due to television, devices and electronic gadgets.

   B Life is competitive nowadays so children need to be pushed to keep up.

   C Silence and time to do nothing give the brain time to make thoughtful decisions rather than act impulsively.

   D Parents schedule children's time to maximise learning and achievement.

Identifying additional evidence that strengthens an argument

2 Permafrost is a frozen layer on the Earth's surface. Climate change is causing the permafrost in the Arctic region in northern Russia and Canada to thaw, releasing vast amounts of methane and carbon dioxide (greenhouse gases) into the atmosphere. This worsens climate change.

We need to keep that methane and carbon dioxide trapped in the permafrost. In past millennia the woolly mammoth trampled the snow, allowing cold air to reach the ground keeping the permafrost at zero degrees. The woolly mammoth is extinct so scientists are releasing bison into areas of permafrost to do the job of the woolly mammoth. Early signs seem to show that this plan is having some success.

Which one of these statements, if true, most strengthens the above argument?

A Some scientists have a radical plan that involves cloning the woolly mammoth and reintroducing the species to the Arctic.

B Scientists predict that 37% of the permafrost could be protected by bison and other herbivores.

C Roads and other infrastructure are built across permafrost so thawing causes extra problems in addition to climate change.

D Thawing permafrost will lead to rising ocean levels across the earth.

Identifying additional evidence that weakens an argument

- When someone makes a claim or presents an argument, they use reasons or evidence to convince others to accept that claim.
- Any statement that calls into question or contradicts any of the evidence used to support a claim or argument will weaken that claim or argument.
- First read the text carefully and identify the claim being made and the supporting evidence for that claim. Then assess which of the statements provided undermines or contradicts the supporting evidence or gives a reason why the claim is not valid.
- Look for the following:
  - a statement that contradicts evidence in the claim
  - a statement that undermines the accuracy of the claim
  - a statement that limits the scope of the claim
  - a statement that makes the claim less likely to hold up.
- When working out your answer, eliminate the options that are incorrect until you find the one that is correct.

SAMPLE QUESTION

Aisha and Cameron have been studying all weekend for an exam on Monday.

Aisha: 'I need to relax. Let's leave the books for a bit and go for a quick walk outside. We can study more when we get back.'
Cameron: 'No way! It's getting hard to concentrate so we can't stop now. We must keep working.'

Which one of these statements, if true, most weakens Cameron's argument?

A It has been shown that fresh air increases your energy.

B Research shows that taking short breaks increases your ability to focus.

C It's raining and cold outside and Cameron does not have a raincoat.

D Walking gets your heart pumping and is a good way to alleviate stress.

B is correct. Cameron argues that they must not take a break because they need to keep working in order to concentrate. The statement that research shows taking short breaks increases your ability to focus most weakens this argument because it contradicts it. If taking short breaks increases your ability to focus, then the fact that it is getting hard to concentrate does not hold up as a reason not to take a break.

A is incorrect. This statement could strengthen a general argument in favour of taking a break and getting some fresh air. Therefore it could weaken Cameron's argument that they must not take a break but it does not **most** weaken his argument.

C is incorrect. This statement might weaken Aisha's argument to go for a walk at that moment but it doesn't weaken Cameron's argument that they mustn't take a break because they need to keep working in order to concentrate.

D is incorrect. This statement strengthens Aisha's argument in favour of taking a break and going for a walk so she can relax. It does not weaken Cameron's argument that they must keep working in order to concentrate.

Identifying additional evidence that weakens an argument

 Practice questions

1 The school principal announced in the assembly that the school would not be replacing the asphalt behind the canteen with a kitchen garden. 'A kitchen garden would be much more costly to set up than simply repairing the current asphalt,' she said. 'A kitchen garden is also more time consuming to maintain. So it is clear that establishing a kitchen garden would be of little value to our school.'

Which one of these statements, if true, most weakens the principal's argument?

A A garden offers many opportunities to learn, including valuable life skills.

B A kitchen garden requires regular upkeep, including planting and weeding.

C Students were surveyed to find the most popular ideas for using the area.

D The school already has an established kitchen garden in another area.

2 Finn's mum thinks that every holiday for the family should be a campervan holiday. 'I like the freedom,' she says. 'Campervanning is just so flexible. We don't have to plan everything. We can just go wherever we want and then pack up and move on to a new location whenever we want to.'

Which one of these statements, if true, most weakens Finn's mum's argument?

A Finn suffers from carsickness and must always sit next to an open window.

B It's relaxing sitting outside the campervan in the evening while the younger kids are asleep.

C Finn has been saving so he will have his own spending money on the next family holiday.

D There are strict rules about where campervans can pitch and most sites require you to book ahead.

☞ **Answers and explanations on page 75**

Identifying an argument that uses the same structure

- Arguments can be structured in various ways, including as follows:
  - They can begin with a thesis statement or claim and then provide evidence to convince others to accept this claim.
  - They can provide evidence then conclude with a claim, a summing-up statement or a call to action.
  - They can include a sequence of evidence with the strongest evidence listed first. Some evidence might tie in clearly to the argument. Other evidence might not so clearly link to the argument.
  - They can state a claim, provide evidence then restate the claim or make a call to action.
- To answer questions where you are asked to identify matching argument structures, you first need to identify the structure of the argument in the box. You don't need to match the topic of the argument or decide whether or not you agree with it. The topic is irrelevant.
- Read the text carefully. Identify the structure of the argument then consider the answer options. Look for the option that matches. Try to quickly eliminate answers that are definitely incorrect.

SAMPLE QUESTION

Manish: 'Nachos are my favourite food. I love nachos with guacamole, jalapenos and melted cheese on top.'

Which argument uses the same structure as the above argument?

A **Selena:** 'I prefer pizza to nachos but I love anything with melted cheese.'

B **Simon:** 'I don't eat cheese because I'm allergic to dairy.'

C **Ivy:** 'Nachos are not my favourite food. I don't like avocado or jalapenos and I don't eat cheese either.'

D **Alex:** 'I make vegan nachos and I use cashews to make vegan cheese. My nachos are the best!'

C is correct. In the argument, Manish gives an opinion and then lists three reasons to support it. In this statement, Ivy gives an opinion and three reasons to support that opinion.

A is incorrect. Selena only gives one reason to support her claim for preferring pizza to nachos.

B is incorrect. Simon only gives one reason to support his statement that he doesn't eat cheese.

D is incorrect. Alex lists the ingredients used to make nachos with the inference that these ingredients make Alex's nachos the best.

Practice questions

1 Jessica said: 'Sebastian wants to become a paramedic. In order for this to happen, he must study hard at university but studying will not be enough. To become a paramedic he will need to be caring, empathetic, a good communicator, a quick thinker, able to remain calm and work under pressure and he must be able to work as a team member. If he does not have the right personal attributes, he will never be able to be a paramedic even if he studies hard.'

Which of these arguments has the same structure as the above argument?

A **Danielle:** 'I usually make a great apple pie. I use green apples and my homemade shortcrust pastry. For the crust to work out I have to roll the ingredients and then refrigerate them for half an hour before rolling the pastry flat. If I don't refrigerate it, it becomes sticky and difficult to work with and the pie crust doesn't work out well.'

B **Raphael**: 'Companion planting is a useful strategy for a vegetable garden. It involves planting specific plants in close proximity to one another for reasons such as pest control, being able to lure insects for pollination and to allow for the space requirements of different plants. Some herbs are great companion plants because they repel insects and attract pollinators. A good example of companion planting is to plant carrots, tomatoes and onions with dill. Dill is a herb that attracts lady beetles which will eat any aphids that could destroy your vegetable plants.'

Identifying an argument that uses the same structure

C **Molly:** 'Praveena hopes to become a successful magician. To become a successful magician she'll need to practise and have the ability and imagination to invent her own tricks. She'll also need to have the confidence to perform for members of the public.'

D **Phoebe**: 'When it comes to hibernation, people generally only think of grizzly bears in North America but Australia has hibernating animals too. In Australia, animals that hibernate include the pygmy possum, some bat species and the short-beaked echidna. The pygmy possum has the world's longest hibernation because it can hibernate for a year'.

2 The Royal National Park, located in the Sutherland Shire in Sydney, is the second-oldest National Park in the world after Yellowstone in the USA. The Royal National Park is a great park to visit. There are many beautiful walking tracks and cycling trails.

Which of the following arguments has the same structure as the above argument?

A Climate change is causing weather patterns around the globe to change in various ways. Heavy rainfall is becoming more frequent globally and this will worsen in many parts of the world, leading to more frequent and more severe flooding events. Some parts of the world will have less rain than usual and this will have a disastrous impact on agriculture in those areas.

B Cane toads are a huge problem in Australia. Cane toads were introduced here as a biological control. A biological control is a method by which humans use a natural enemy to control an invasive species. A biological control needs to be carefully considered before it is introduced to the environment because it can cause a bigger problem than the one it's meant to fix. Cane toads were introduced as a biological control to eat the sugar-cane beetles that were destroying sugar-cane crops but now cane toads are a bigger problem than the cane beetles were because cane toads have no natural enemies to control their population.

C Drought affects the length and quality of the ski season at ski resorts in Australia because there is less snow but also, during a drought, there is less water available to make snow using snow machines.

D The tiny 3-cm-long Nursery frog that lives on a mountain top in the Daintree Rainforest in North Queensland is at risk of extinction because of climate change. The frog needs to stay cool and wet but climate change has led to increases in temperature that reduce the moisture and cloud cover in the frog's mountain environment, making it too warm and dry for the tiny frog to survive.

Ordering items in one way

- When answering questions of this kind, the statements given will tell you the positions but in a very roundabout way.
- In the sample below, the first statement is 'No one arrives back before Ava'. What does this mean in terms of her position in the race? This is just telling you that Ava came first.
- If you need to, jot down the first letter of each person or object in the order you think they are and check this against the statement before answering.

SAMPLE QUESTION

Ava, Benjamin, Chloe, and Daniel are four students who had a swimming race to see who could swim around a boat and return to shore first.

- No-one arrived back before Ava.
- Two people were faster than Benjamin.
- Benjamin arrived back before Daniel.

Where did Chloe finish?

A first

B second

C third

D fourth

B is correct.
If no-one arrived before Ava, she came first. If two people were ahead of Benjamin, he came third. Daniel was slower than Benjamin so he came fourth. Chloe must have come in second.

 Practice questions

1. Javier, Kara, Miriam, Yaz and Zachary are five students who had a spelling bee to see who could spell the most words correctly.

   Javier finished ahead of Zachary, who finished two places ahead of Yaz.

   If Miriam also finished ahead of Zachary, where did Kara finish?

   A first

   B second

   C fourth

   D fifth

2. Elena, Felix, Grace and Henry are four friends who had a cooking competition to see who could bake the best chocolate cake. Another friend judged the competition purely on how the cakes tasted.

   Felix's cake was tastier than Grace's but not as tasty as Henry's.

   Nobody had a tastier cake than Elena.

   Who baked the least tasty cake?

   A Elena

   B Felix

   C Grace

   D Henry

Ordering items in two ways

- When a list of items or people can be ordered in more than one way, it is often best to break down the information and focus only on one way of ordering at a time.
- In the following example you are required to answer questions about the value of paintings and sculptures owned by four people.
- First focus on the statements about the paintings. Can you order the people solely on the value of their paintings?
- Once you have done this you can focus on the statements about the sculptures to answer the question.

SAMPLE QUESTION

Liam, Sophia, Benjamin, and Emily are four friends. Each friend has a unique and valuable collection of paintings and sculptures.

- Liam's paintings are more valuable than Benjamin's but his sculptures are worth less.
- Sophia's paintings are worth less than Benjamin's but her sculptures are worth more than Emily's sculptures.
- Emily's sculptures are worth more than Benjamin's but her paintings are worth less than Sophia's.

The person who has the most valuable collection of paintings also has:

A the most valuable sculptures.

B the second-most valuable sculptures.

C the third-most valuable sculptures.

D the least valuable sculptures.

D is correct.

You must first find the person with the most valuable painting collection.

Liam's paintings are worth more than Benjamin's, whose paintings are worth more than Sophia's. Emily's paintings are worth less than Sophia's so Liam has the most valuable collection of paintings.

Now you must find out what value Liam's sculptures have.

Liam's sculptures are worth less than Benjamin's. Sophia's sculptures are worth more than Emily's, whose sculptures are worth more than Benjamin's. This means Liam's sculptures are worth the least.

Practice questions

1. Adrian, Ella, Mateo and Sophie are four friends who enter paintings into an art competition. The paintings are scored in two ways. They are scored on the artist's technique and for creativity.
   - Ella scored higher than Mateo in technique but lower in creativity.
   - Adrian scored higher for creativity than Ella and Mateo.
   - Sophie scored lower than Ella for creativity but higher in technique.
   - Adrian scored higher than Mateo but lower than Ella for technique.

   The person who scored first for creativity finished in which position for technique?

   A first

   B second

   C third

   D fourth

2. Charlie, Javi, Liam and Shristi are four athletes participating in a track-and-field event. They are competing in the 100-m sprint and the long jump. They are the only four competitors.
   - The person who came last in the sprint came second in the long jump.
   - The person who came first in the sprint came last in the long jump.
   - Shristi didn't come first or last in either of the events.
   - Liam finished both events in the position immediately in front of Javi.

   Who won the long jump?

   A Charlie

   B Javi

   C Liam

   D Shristi

Answers and explanations on page 76

Questions using 3D puzzles

- Solving three-dimensional (3D) puzzles on paper can be difficult. Learning how 3D objects can be rotated in your hands is important so playing with blocks and Lego is very useful.
- When solving the questions in this book, try to turn pieces over in your head. It is best to turn pieces over in line with the sides of the piece. Pretend you have stuck a skewer through the shape and turned it around that. What happens to each part of it? If there is a sloped part, where will that end up?
- How wide is the shape? How tall?
- Sometimes it is easier to turn one piece than another over in your head, so try turning the object in the question if you can't turn the objects in the answers.

SAMPLE QUESTION

The following solid is part of a 3D puzzle.

Which of the following solids will fit with the piece above to make a cube?

A   B

C   D

C is correct.
If you turn over the solid in C, you can see it fits perfectly over the original piece of the puzzle.

---

1 The following solid is part of a 3D puzzle.

Which of the following solids will fit with the piece above to make a cube?

A   B

C   D

2 The following solid is part of a 3D puzzle.

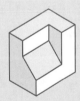

Which of the following solids will fit with the piece above to make a cube?

A   B

C   D

Questions about nets and dice

- To prepare for questions about nets of dice, it is a good idea to cut out some nets yourself and fold them up.
- Find out which faces of a net will be next to each other and which faces will be opposite each other. For example, two faces will be on opposite sides of a dice if they are separated by one face and are connected in a straight line.
- When the faces of dice are images, take note of important features. If there are arrows, to which face of the dice is it pointing? Which face of the dice is it attached to on the side?

SAMPLE QUESTION

The following is one view of a six-sided dice.

Which of the following is **not** a possible net of the dice?

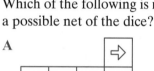

A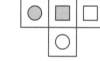

B

C

D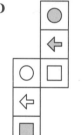

B is correct.

When B is folded to make the dice and the purple square is facing up, the white arrow would be on the left side if the white square was also visible. This is shown on the right.

In the view of the dice shown in the question, the arrow is on the right side.

Similarly if the net was folded and the squares were in the same place, the dice would show the purple circle in the space meant to be showing the arrow.

Practice questions

1 The following is one view of a six-sided dice.

Which of the following is **not** a possible net of the dice?

A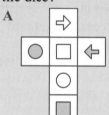

B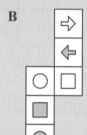

C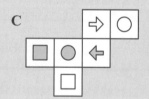

D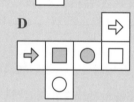

2 The following is the net of a six-sided dice.

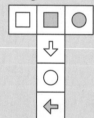

Which of the following is a possible view of the dice?

A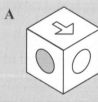

B

C

D

Ordering items based on many factors

- These are often the most difficult questions as a lot of information is given and must be taken into account. Reading the information carefully is important.
- Often it is best to sketch a very basic table to keep track of all your working. You don't need to make tables as detailed as the ones in the explanations in this book. First initials are usually fine as names will usually all start with different letters. In the sample question below, you can start by listing the numbers 1, 2, 3, 4 and 5 in order.
- Read the information once to see which bits tell you something you can immediately put down. For example, in the sample question below, the third statement tells you Victor was in room 4. You can put a V under the number 4 straightaway.
- Then reread the information as many times as necessary for you to continue putting information down until you can see your way to the answer.
- These questions may take longer than others but don't rush them.

SAMPLE QUESTION

Ryan, Samuel, Thomas, Uma and Victor checked into a motel using rooms 1, 2, 3, 4 and 5. The rooms are all in a row. Each person then ordered a different meal for breakfast the next morning, to be delivered to their rooms.

- Ryan was in the room next door to Samuel, who ordered porridge.
- Thomas ordered a boiled egg.
- Victor was in room 4 and was next door to the person who ordered fruit salad.
- Thomas and Victor were not next door to each other.
- The person in room 5 ordered an omelette.

Who checked into room 2?

A Ryan   **B** Samuel   **C** Thomas   **D** Uma

B is correct.
Victor was in room 4. The person in room 5 ordered an omelette and the person in room 3 ordered a fruit salad. Ryan and Samuel are next to each other so they must be in rooms 2 and 3 because Thomas, who ordered an egg, cannot be next to Victor, and so must be in room 1. As the person in room 3 ordered fruit salad, it cannot

have been Samuel as he ordered porridge. The people are split into the rooms as shown.

Room	1	2	3	4	5
Person	Thomas	Samuel	Ryan	Victor	Uma
Breakfast	egg	porridge	fruit salad		omelette

Samuel checked into room 2.

Practice questions

1. Madison, Nora, Owen, Paige and Queenie are the five finalists in a fashion-design competition. They each designed a dress of a different colour. There was one black, one white, one pink, one green and one orange dress.
   - Madison was awarded third place for her dress.
   - The green dress was awarded fifth place.
   - Paige designed the pink dress and she didn't come first or second.
   - Nora finished one place ahead of Queenie, who made the black dress.
   - The orange dress was judged to be better than the white dress.

   Who made the white dress?
   A Madison   **B** Nora
   C Owen   **D** Queenie

2. F, G, H, I and J are friends. They all have either red or brown hair. They each play two of the following three sports: Aussie rules, soccer or cricket.
   - F plays Aussie rules and cricket.
   - G plays Aussie rules and soccer.
   - H plays soccer.
   - Everyone plays Aussie rules except for one person with red hair.
   - Everyone who plays cricket has the same colour hair.
   - The same number of people play cricket as play soccer.

   What must be true?
   A There are more people with red hair than brown hair.
   B F and G have the same colour hair.
   C C, H and I have the same colour hair.
   D J plays cricket.

☞ Answers and explanations on page 77

Questions with stencils

- This type of question tests your ability to visualise the combinations of shapes as they interact with each other.
- For the questions in this book it is usually the case that the innermost colour is on the first square of colour. It is also mostly true that the outermost colour is the last square of paper in the process.
- The confusing thing about questions like this is that you might see a grey shape in the final image that isn't one of the pieces of paper you can use. This is because the image is made from what is cut out of a piece of paper and the colour underneath is what you can see.
- Take these questions slowly; often the answer goes against your first intuition.

SAMPLE QUESTION

Here are some square pieces of paper. They are labelled with numbers and some of them have holes cut out of them.

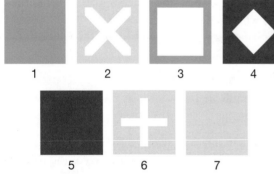

The following image was made by placing four of these pieces on top of each other in a particular order.

What is the order in which the pieces were placed down?

A 1, 4, 6, 3

B 5, 6, 4, 3

C 5, 4, 6, 3

D 1, 2, 4, 3

B is correct.

The order in which the squares should be placed down is shown below, as is the pile after each square is added.

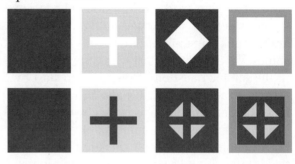

Practice questions

1 Here are some square pieces of paper. They are labelled with numbers and some of them have holes cut out of them.

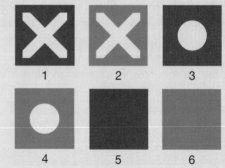

The following image was made by placing three of these pieces on top of each other in a particular order.

In which order were the pieces placed down?

A 5, 4, 1

B 6, 3, 1

C 5, 2, 3

D 6, 1, 3

☞ Answers and explanations on page 77

2 Here are some square pieces of paper. They are labelled with numbers and some of them have holes cut out of them.

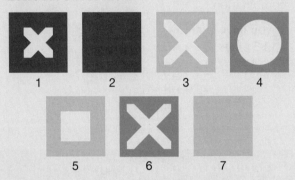

The following image was made by placing four of these pieces on top of each other in a particular order.

What is the order in which the pieces were placed down?

A   2, 5, 6, 3

B   2, 5, 4, 3

C   7, 1, 6, 3

D   7, 4, 1, 3

Questions that use multiplication

- There are many questions that use multiplication. However, the questions below rely on your ability to multiply something more than once and by different numbers.
- For this reason it is very important to know your multiplication tables.
- In these questions it can also be useful to use trial and error to find the correct answer. You will notice that often you are given a total number of items—coloured tokens, for example. You may not know how many of each token you have but you may know you have fewer of one token than the others.
- Start with one of the tokens of which you have fewest. Does this give you the right number of total tokens? If not, try with two of that token. Work your way up until you come across the correct combination of tokens.
- This method is possible because most of this question type will not include too many large numbers.

SAMPLE QUESTION

In a game that uses plastic tokens to represent points, the green tokens are worth 2 points, the blue tokens are worth 5 points and the yellow tokens are worth 10 points.

I have twice as many green tokens as yellow tokens. I have three more blue tokens than green tokens.

If I have 13 tokens in total, how many points do I have?

A 58

B 63

C 72

D 79

B is correct.

You need to find out how many there are of each colour token. Knowing there are only 13 tokens in total means you can easily use trial and error. The yellow tokens are fewest as there are twice as many greens and there are three more blues than greens.

If you have 1 yellow, you will have 2 greens and 5 blues: $1 + 2 + 5 = 8$, not 13 so this cannot be the combination.

If you have 2 yellows, you will have 4 greens and 7 blues: $2 + 4 + 7 = 13$ tokens.

Total points $= 2 \times 10 + 4 \times 2 + 7 \times 5$
$= 20 + 8 + 35$
$= 63$ points

Practice questions

1 Carlos has some 20c, 50c and $1 coins in his pocket. He has the same number of each coin. If two types (denominations) of coins are worth $7.20, how much money does he have altogether?

A $10.20

B $10.70

C $11.20

D $11.70

2 Bella collects sports cards but doesn't open the packs as she doesn't want to damage the cards inside. They come in packs of 4, 10 or 15. She has four times as many packs of 4 as she does packs of 15. She has three more packs of 10 than she does packs of 4.

Bella has 30 packs altogether. How many cards does she have?

A 243

B 264

C 290

D 302

   ☞ Answers and explanations on page 77

Questions that involve switching symbols

- Questions that involve long strings of symbols, codes or switches are often found in thinking skills tests.
- It is important to take note of how symbols change. In the sample question below, shapes change to other shapes in a particular pattern. In some other questions, switches turn on or off.
- For the questions below, it can be useful to lightly sketch the shape that one will change to. This may help you identify where you might find particular strings of symbols.

SAMPLE QUESTION

The following string of shapes is part of a game.

A single move consists of a player tapping two consecutive shapes. The shapes that are tapped will change in the following way:

- A square will turn into a triangle.
- A triangle will turn into a circle.
- A circle will turn into a square.

Which of the following is it **not** possible to see inside the string after only one move?

A □ ○ ○ ○

B □ △ △ △

C ○ ○ ○ △

D □ □ □ ○

B is correct.
It is possible to find A inside the string if either of the following two selections are made.

□ ○ ○ △ △ □ □ ○ △ △

It is possible to find C inside the string if the two shapes selected are tapped.

□ ○ ○ △ △ □ □ ○ △ △

It is possible to find D inside the string if the two shapes selected are tapped.

□ ○ ○ △ □ □ ○ △ △

The only way to get three triangles in a row is by changing the shapes selected. This leaves a circle as the shape to the left of the triangles. B is not possible.

□ ○ ○ △ □ □ ○ △ △

🖉 Practice questions

1 The string of symbols below are shown on a screen as part of a game.

Δ Ω Ψ Ψ Δ Ω Ω Δ Ψ Δ

During the game a player must make at least one move. A single move consists of tapping two consecutive symbols. The symbols that are tapped change in the following way:

- A Δ becomes a Ψ
- A Ψ becomes a Ω
- A Ω becomes a Δ

Looking at the string of symbols, a player makes only one move. Which of the following is it **not** possible to see inside the string after only one move?

A   Δ Δ Δ Δ   B   Δ Δ Ψ Δ
C   Ψ Δ Ψ Ψ   D   Δ Δ Ω Δ

2 Six light switches start in the positions shown.

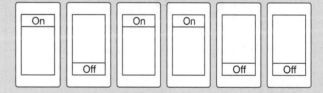

Pablo is challenged by his friend to turn all the switches off. However, the challenge is made difficult because he must always flick two switches at the same time. This is considered one move. Can he turn all the switches off and, if so, how many moves will it take him?

A   No, it cannot be done.

B   Yes, in 2 moves

C   Yes, in 3 moves

D   Yes, in 5 moves

Questions that involve two sides of a card

- These questions test your ability to work out what is hidden from you just by looking at one side of a card.
- The key to solving these problems is knowing that if two numbers, letters or symbols are on the two sides of a card, then they cannot be seen together. That is, you cannot see two sides of a card at the same time.
- Work out how many individual letters or numbers are used and list them. This helps when it comes to eliminating the possible combinations on each card.
- Each question uses a process of elimination to find the answer.

SAMPLE QUESTION

I have three cards. Each card has a letter printed on each side. No letter appears twice on the cards. The cards can be set out to show the three words below:

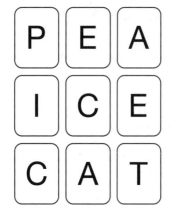

Which other word can the cards be used to spell out?

A CAP

B PET

C TIP

D TEA

C is correct. It is possible to make the word TIP.

There are three cards with two sides. So there are six letters in all: A, C, E, I, P and T. If two letters are on the same card, they cannot both appear in the same word.

The letter C cannot be on the same card as the I, E, A or T because it is in the words ICE and CAT. It must be on the same card as the P. So CAP cannot be made by the cards. Option A is incorrect.

The letter E cannot be on the same card as the A or the I because it is in the words PEA and ICE. It must be on the same card as the T. So both PET and TEA are not possible. Options B and D are incorrect.

The letters A and I are on the same card.

🖉 Practice questions

1 I have three cards. Each card has a letter printed on each side. No letter appears twice on the cards. The cards can be set out to show the three words below:

Which other word can the cards be used to spell out?

A WET   **B** NEW   **C** ANT   **D** EAR

2 The numbers 1 to 8 are written randomly on the front and back of four cards. Each card has one number on each side. Each card has a value that is the sum of the two numbers written on it. For example, a card that has a 1 on one side and a 2 on the other would have a value of 3.

Of the four cards, one has a value of 13, one has a value of 12 and one has a value of 7.

What number is on the same card as the 5?

A 2   **B** 3   **C** 7   **D** 8

Questions involving area

- The area of a shape is the amount of space it takes up in two dimensions.
- Once again, multiplication skills are important, as is the ability to convert between metres and centimetres.
- It is not necessary to actually calculate areas but you will need to calculate how many of one shape will fit into another.
- Use the shape given in the question to help you find the answer. Can it be split in a way that will help you? Or can you use a number of these shapes to cover an area that is easier to work with?
- Some area questions will ask you to work with repeated patterns or tiles. To fit into the floor area of a room, tiles may be cut into smaller shapes. For example, if a tile 50 cm wide is used on an area 1.75 m by 1.25 m, some tiles will need to be cut as shown in the following diagram.

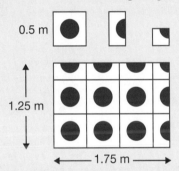

- Notice that the tile used in the top-right corner is cut vertically and horizontally to make it fit.

SAMPLE QUESTION

The following tile is used to cover the floor of a bathroom that measures 2.3 m by 2.3 m.

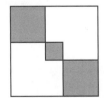

The tile is a square of side length 50 cm.

In the bottom-left corner of the room is a full tile. What tile will sit in the top right corner of the room?

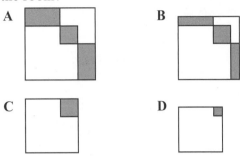

C is correct.

The corner piece must be a 30-cm by 30-cm square. Looking at the diagram below, we can see how the tiles will fit across the room.

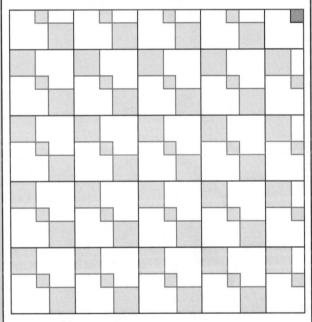

Look at the full 50-cm tile and work out where 30 cm is along the side of it. Looking at the diagram below, you can see where that is.

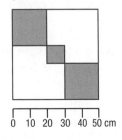

Questions involving area

 Practice questions

1 The following tile is used to cover a rectangular area measuring 1.25 m by 1 m.

The tile measures 25 cm by 15 cm.

The tiles are laid down next to each other so that the edges line up.

If the long side of the tile runs along the long side of the rectangular area, which of the following tiles will also be used?

A

B

C

D

2 Mitchell is a gardener with a number of lawns to mow today. He mows lawns at a constant speed. The first lawn he must mow is a rectangle with side lengths 20 m and 40 m. He starts this at 9 am and finishes at 9:30 am. He starts the next lawn at 10 am.

If this next lawn is a rectangle with dimensions 40 m by 80 m, what time will he finish mowing it?

A 10:30 am

B 11 am

C 11:30 am

D 12 noon

☞ **Answers and explanations on page 78**

20 MIN

1 Ivy, Jacques, Lily and Magnus are four athletes who competed in the discus. They were the only competitors.

- Jacques threw further than only one other athlete.
- Ivy was beaten by only one other athlete.
- Magnus threw further than Lily.

Who won the competition?

A Ivy

B Jacques

C Lily

D Magnus

2 Berries are very healthy. Nutritionists recommend eating half a cup a day to prevent heart disease and Alzheimer's. The problem with this recommendation for many people is that berries can be quite expensive and many people cannot afford to eat berries every day, especially out of season. The government should subsidise berries so that people can eat them on a daily basis to improve their health and prevent disease.

Which statement strengthens the above argument?

A Investing in preventative health measures saves money because it's easier and cheaper to prevent disease than treat it.

B Governments cannot afford to subsidise berries for people who want to eat them because that would cost the economy too much.

C Governments get their money from taxpayers and taxpayers will never agree to subsidise the cost of berries.

D Berries are good for your health.

3 In a survey of aged-care residents about their preferences of flowers for the community gardens, everyone who liked succulents liked cacti and everyone who liked cacti liked banksia but no-one who liked cacti liked roses.

Ethel, Aggie, Doris and Jorge all took part in the survey.

Based on the given information, which of the following must be true?

A If Ethel likes banksia, she also likes cacti.

B If Jorge likes succulents, he does not like roses.

C If Doris does not like succulents, she does not like cacti.

D If Aggie likes roses, she does not like banksia.

4 The following solid is part of a 3D puzzle.

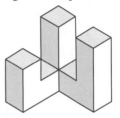

Which of the following solids will fit with the piece above to make a cube?

A

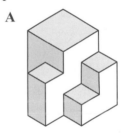

B

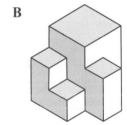

C

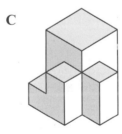

D

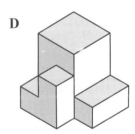

5 **Xanthe:** Our car can travel 320 km on a full charge. Your car is smaller so you must get more kilometres than us on a full charge.

James: No, that's not right. Our car might get fewer kilometres than yours on a charge.

If the above information is true, whose reasoning is correct?

A Xanthe only

B James only

C Both Xanthe and James

D Neither Xanthe nor James

6 Here are some square pieces of paper. They are labelled with numbers and some of them have holes cut out of them.

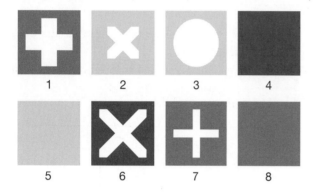

1 2 3 4

5 6 7 8

The following image was made by placing four of these pieces on top of each other in a particular order.

In which order were the pieces placed?

A 4, 2, 1, 3
B 8, 2, 6, 3
C 5, 7, 6, 3
D 5, 6, 1, 3

7 Kiara is counting her cash after a day selling items at a market stall. She has a number of $5, $10, $20 and $50 notes.

She has three times as many $20 notes as she does $50 notes. She has two more $10 notes than $20 notes. If these three denominations make up 16 notes and Kiara has $325 in total, how many $5 notes does she have?

A 1
B 5
C 9
D 11

8 Todd's family has four horses: Roxie, Lulu, Honey and Tigger. Todd has worked out each horse's favourite treats. He has found that if a horse likes apples, it also likes carrots and if it likes carrots, it also likes dates. No horse that likes carrots also likes raisins.

Based on the above information, which of the statements below must be true?

A If Roxie likes raisins, she also likes apples.
B If Lulu does not like raisins, she also does not like carrots.
C If Honey likes dates, she must like apples.
D If Tigger doesn't like apples, she also doesn't like carrots.

9 Helen's school completed a survey about student screen time before bed. The survey found that students who use electronic devices before bed had more difficulty falling asleep than students who read printed books at bedtime.

Helen: The results show that using electronic devices does not help you get to sleep.

Which of the following statements shows the mistake Helen has made?

A It could be that students are using devices because they cannot get to sleep.
B It could be that students who don't use devices at bedtime spend more time watching television.
C It could be that some students are not allowed to use devices at bedtime.
D It could be that some students are more interested than others in electronic devices.

☞ Answers and explanations on pages 79–81

10 Seven light switches start in the positions shown.

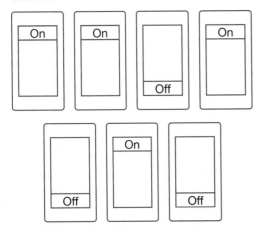

Gustav is challenged by his friend to turn all the switches to 'Off'. However, the challenge is made more difficult because his friend says he must always flick three switches at the same time. This is considered one move. What is the minimum number of moves it will take to turn all the light switches to 'Off'?

A 1

B 2

C 3

D 4

11 Sonja says: 'In Australia, we should mostly grow hazelnuts instead of almonds. Almond trees require a great deal of water. Almond crops should only be grown in areas of Australia where water is plentiful so that irrigators don't take water from rivers that is needed further down the river system for other farms and for the general environment. Almonds are not sustainable in many parts of Australia.'

Which statement weakens Sonja's argument?

A Almonds are a healthy food.

B Almond trees grow well in some wetter parts of Australia.

C People prefer the taste of almonds to hazelnuts.

D Hazelnuts require minimal water and survive in fertile soils.

12 Four friends were discussing their preferences for pop, rock and rap music.

- Ash likes rap better than rock.
- Only Gitte likes pop more than rock.
- Hilda and Ben both like rap more than pop.
- No-one likes rock least.

If the above information is correct, which of the following **cannot** be true?

A Three people liked rap best.

B No-one liked rap best.

C No-one liked pop least.

D Hilda and Ben liked pop least.

13 All badminton players need to attend two practice sessions per week or they risk being dropped from the team. They might also be dropped if they have not been playing as well as others on the team.

Kirsty: Bianca was dropped from the team even though she's been playing well. She must not have been at the two training sessions this week.

Amy: If Bianca attended practice and improved her performance, she would definitely not be dropped from the team.

If the above information is true, whose reasoning is correct?

A Kirsty only

B Amy only

C Both Kirsty and Amy

D Neither Kirsty nor Amy

14 I have three cards. Each card has a letter printed on each side. No letter appears twice on the cards. The cards can be set out to show the three words below:

Which word below **cannot** be spelt out using the cards?

A LEG

B PEG

C GAP

D ALE

15 The following is the net of a six-sided dice.

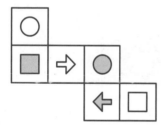

Which of the following is **not** a view of the dice?

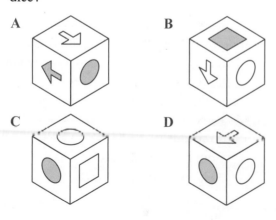

16 The Monarch butterfly has one of the longest migration journeys in the animal kingdom: over 4000 kilometres from Canada to Mexico. The Monarch eats milkweed leaves and only lays its eggs on milkweed plants. In North America, deforestation and extreme weather events due to climate change are wiping out milkweed. Without ample food and breeding grounds the butterflies can't survive.

The Monarch is not a native species in Australia but arrived with milkweed plants in 1871. In Australia the Monarch makes a shorter migration but lack of food is also endangering the Monarch in Australia.

Which statement best expresses the main idea of the text?

A The Monarch is not a native species in Australia.

B Without ample food the butterflies can't survive.

C The Monarch butterfly has one of the longest migration journeys in the animal kingdom.

D Monarch butterflies are under threat of extinction due to habitat loss.

17 Emma, Lukas, Maya and Xavier are four participants who finished first, second, third and fourth in a chess competition. They can be ordered by the overall position they achieved and by the average time it took them to win each game.

- Emma finished ahead of Lukas but behind Maya.
- Lukas finished ahead of Xavier but each win took him longer.
- Maya won games faster than Xavier but slower than Emma.

What was the position of the person who took the shortest time to win each game?

A first

B second

C third

D fourth

☞ Answers and explanations on pages 79–81

18 Grandma Dorothy has been living in an aged-care facility for two years and usually has a good relationship with her carer. Lately Tim has noticed that Grandma Dorothy is grumpy and short tempered. Tim has decided to request a different carer for his grandmother.

What is Tim's assumption?

A He should ask Grandma Dorothy what is bothering her.

B Grandma Dorothy would like a new carer.

C Her carer must be the cause of Grandma's grumpiness and short temper.

D Grandma must be unhappy about something at the aged-care facility.

19 A rectangular room 2.9 m wide and 3.85 m long is to be covered by the square carpet tiles below that are 0.5 m by 0.5 m.

If one corner contains a full tile that touches both walls, which of the following tiles will fit in the opposite corner?

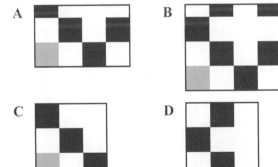

20 Five bands performed one after the other at a competition and the best three were awarded prizes. The bands were named Alpha Tauri, Bravo Billy, Cheeky Charlies, Delta Force and Echo Point.

- Alpha Tauri performed straight after Delta Force.
- Bravo Billy performed second.
- Cheeky Charlies didn't perform first or last.
- First prize was awarded to the band that performed fourth.
- The band that performed first won a prize.
- The band that won third prize performed straight after the band that got second prize.

What prize did the Cheeky Charlies win?

A first

B second

C third

D no prize

1 Mick, Nyjah, Ollie, Preston and Quinton entered a skateboarding competition. They were the only competitors.

Nyjah finished ahead of Preston but exactly two places behind Ollie.

If Mick finished ahead of Ollie, in what place did Quinton finish?

A first

B third

C fourth

D fifth

2 The following solid is part of a 3D puzzle.

Which of the following solids will fit with the piece above to make a cube?

A

B

C

D

3 In the nation of Buckistan, there are four types of coin. There are 2 ammas to 1 bamma, 5 cammas to 1 damma and 25 bammas to 1 damma.

How many ammas are there in 1 camma?

A 5

B 10

C 25

D 50

4 Peter and Jordan are brothers. Their parents have told them they won't be allowed to go to Georgia's birthday party if they haven't finished their homework.

Safin: Peter is coming to the party but Jordan isn't so Jordan can't have finished his homework.

Daniel: Peter must have finished his homework.

If the information in the box is true, whose reasoning is correct?

A Safin only

B Daniel only

C Both Safin and Daniel

D Neither Safin nor Daniel

5 Sophia wants to join the choir. To qualify she must first attend the audition.

Jackson: I know Sophia attended the audition on Monday so she'll definitely be chosen for the choir.

Which of the following shows the mistake Jackson has made?

A Sophia might not want to join the choir.

B The choir might not be accepting new singers.

C Attendance at the audition might not be the only criterion for joining the choir.

D Sophia might not have attended the audition after all.

SAMPLE TEST 1B

6 Here are some square pieces of paper. They are labelled with numbers and some of them have holes cut out of them.

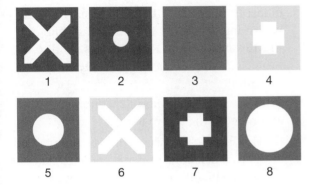

1   2   3   4

5   6   7   8

The following image was made by placing four of these pieces on top of each other in a particular order.

What is the order in which the pieces were placed?

A 3, 4, 1, 8

B 3, 6, 7, 8

C 3, 1, 4, 8

D 3, 7, 6, 8

7 Dave set up the party lights for the school disco. He has blue, yellow, white and red lights connected to three switches. When a switch is pressed, all the lights it controls turn on or off. Only one switch can be on at a time.

Switch 1 controls red and white lights only.

Switch 2 controls red, white and blue lights only.

Switch 3 controls blue and yellow lights only.

Which one of the following statements is true?

A It is possible to have all four colours on at the same time.

B The blue light cannot be on when the yellow light is on.

C The white lights cannot be on when the blue lights are on.

D The red lights cannot be on when the white lights are off.

8 A Swiss company is working to prevent climate change. It makes designer handbags and backpacks out of recycled truck tarpaulins, used car airbags and defective materials intended for cars but not acceptable for use. The company sells bags online globally and advertises its role in helping to prevent further climate change by reducing waste and operating 100% sustainably.

Which statement weakens the above argument?

A Recycling used for defective materials in this way reduces landfill.

B The company says their handbags and backpacks are lightweight and durable.

C Shopping locally is part of a sustainable lifestyle and will help prevent further climate change.

D The company is a success story with increasing sales globally.

9 The following string of shapes is part of a game.

A single move consists of a player tapping two consecutive shapes. The shapes that are tapped will change in the following way:

- A square will turn into a triangle.
- A triangle will turn into a circle.
- A circle will turn into a square.

Which of the following is it **not** possible to see inside the string after only one move?

A △△△□

B □□□○

C ○○○△

D □□□△

10

Zane: I saw the police pull over a driver on the motorway. The driver must have been speeding.

Yana: The driver might have been talking on the phone. The police will issue a fine for that too.

Layne: The driver can't have been wearing a seat belt. The police will issue a fine for that as well.

Emily: There are many reasons why the police might have stopped a vehicle but it was most likely for speeding.

Which two people have used correct reasoning?

A Zane and Emily only

B Layne and Emily only

C Zane and Layne only

D Yana and Emily only

11 The numbers 1 to 8 are written randomly on the front and back of four cards. Each card has one number on each side. Each card has a value that is the sum of the two numbers written on it. For example, a card that has a 1 on one side and a 2 on the other would have a value of 3.

Of the four cards, two have a value of 10 and one has a value of 11.

The cards can be arranged to show the number below.

Which other number is it possible to write using these four cards?

A 5623

B 1467

C 8731

D 6843

12 A healthy Martuwarra Fitzroy River is vital for the environment. The river is home to the endangered freshwater sawfish and the river's catchment area is home to one of Australia's oldest flora species: the boab tree. The area is also important for the survival of bilbies. Martuwarra Fitzroy River waters need to be protected from extensive drainage for irrigation.

Which text has the same structure of argument as the above text?

A The spectacled flying fox is an endangered species. Scientific research and First Nations lore highlight the critical role played by the flying fox in the environment. The flying fox is a major pollinator of flowering native plants such as the eucalyptus tree and it disperses seeds as it forages in the forest. These small mammals fly long distances so the seeds they disperse have a better chance of surviving and regenerating forests. The government needs to act to save the spectacled flying fox from extinction.

B Artificial intelligence technology is likely to replace up to half of the workforce by 2030. AI is already common in many aspects of our lives.

C Teff is an ancient grain. It probably originated around 4000 BCE in Ethiopia. Teff is a very important crop in Ethiopia. Many people eat it three times a day and 43% of the country's farmers rely on teff for their income.

D Gratitude is important for health. Being grateful makes people healthier and happier. Try to be grateful for the smallest things: the food you eat, having a bed to sleep in, being able to walk in the fresh air—whatever experiences are available to you. Say thank you. Grateful people tend to take better care of themselves with diet and exercise, and experience lowered levels of stress. Being grateful is good for your health.

☞ Answers and explanations on pages 81–84

13 The following is one view of a six-sided dice.

Which of the following is the only possible net of the dice?

A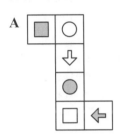

B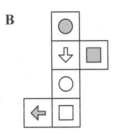

C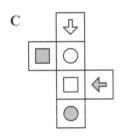

D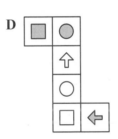

14 Elijah, Fong, Niamh and Siddharth each entered a photo in a photography competition. There were no other competitors. They can receive a prize based on the judges' votes but there is also a prize for the most votes received from the public.

- The person who won the judges' prize came third in the public prize.
- The person who won the public prize came last in the judges' prize.
- The person who came third in the judges' prize came second in the public prize.
- Niamh was beaten by Fong in both prizes.
- Siddharth came second in the public prize.

Who came last in the judges' prize?

A Elijah

B Fong

C Niamh

D Siddharth

15 A train left Melbourne at 5 am to go to Sydney. It travelled at a constant speed for the entire journey and arrived in Sydney at 5 pm the same day.

A different train left Sydney at 10 am on the same day, travelled at the same constant speed and arrived in Melbourne at 10 pm.

At what time did the two trains pass each other?

A 12 noon

B 12:30 pm

C 1:30 pm

D 3:30 pm

16 Travelling in the outdoors can often be too difficult for a person with a disability so some tourism destinations and experiences now provide access through gaming. Virtual travellers with varying degrees of ability can 'log in' to swim with dolphins, hike a mountainside or go caving without having to navigate nature's unpredictability. These travel opportunities bring a wealth of health benefits to people of all abilities and allow people with disabilities to experience travel that's as good as actually being there.

Which of the following statements strengthens the above argument?

A Virtual travel allows you to visit a location before going there so you know what to expect.

B Virtual travel doesn't allow you to interact with the locals or with a travel partner.

C The equipment required for virtual travel is currently very expensive.

D Virtual reality allows people with disabilities to feel in control of their travel experience.

17 Male high-jump trials are being held in Brisbane this week to determine the five or six athletes who will compete in an international competition in Spain in three months. Countries can enter a four-person team for the team competition plus two individual athletes for the individual events.

The top two Australian performers at the Brisbane trials will earn an invitation to compete in the team event in Spain. Three more athletes will be selected by the National Athletics Committee.

Another high jumper, Damon, has already been approved to represent Australia in the individual events in Spain because of how well he has performed internationally over the past three years. Damon will still compete in the Brisbane trials. If he finishes in the top two at the trials, he will automatically enter into the team competition. But that would mean the individual spot he has already earned would be forfeited and the state will send just five men.

Based on the above information, which of the following **cannot** be true?

A Three athletes will be selected by the committee.

B If Damon does not make it into the team competition, then he cannot compete individually.

C Two athletes will be named as individual competitors.

D Damon could compete as an individual competitor based on his own body of work.

18 A blizzard is a snowstorm accompanied by very cold, strong winds. Blizzards can be deadly because of poor visibility. People should not drive in blizzard conditions because of the increased risk of road accidents.

Which of the following statements strengthens the above argument?

A Reduced visibility means it's dangerous to drive in a blizzard.

B Poor visibility means it's more difficult for rescue services to reach car accidents.

C Pedestrians can also be affected by reduced visibility and become disoriented and lost.

D Car pile-ups on motorways leave people stranded in freezing cars for hours.

19 The round-robin athletics competition involves four sports: javelin, discus, long jump and high jump. Competitors can enter the girls' competition, the boys' competition or the mixed-gender competition and compete for individual event trophies or register to compete for the all-round athlete trophies.

To compete for an all-round athlete trophy the competitor must compete in each one of the four sports. Competitors then receive points if they come first, second or third in any of the sports. If a competitor wins a first-place trophy in an individual event, they cannot collect points towards the all-round athlete trophy. Competitors who placed second, third and fourth collect the points.

For example: Robbie, Blake and Gisele are competing for the all-round athlete trophy in the mixed-gender category but Yasmin is not. Yasmin finishes first in the high-jump competition while Robbie finishes second, Blake finishes third and Gisele finishes fourth. Yasmin will be awarded the first-place trophy for the event while Robbie will receive the first-place points toward the all-round athlete trophy. Blake will receive the second-place points and Gisele will receive the third-place points.

Based on the above information, which one of the following **cannot** be true?

A No competitor competing for the all-round athlete trophy won a trophy for the basketball event.

B The competitor with the highest number of points won a trophy for soccer.

C A competitor not competing for the all-round athlete trophy cannot win points for placing first, second or third in an event.

D A club with an outstanding girls' team won the all-round athlete trophy.

SAMPLE TEST 1B

20 Vince is 8 years old. He uses a code when writing to his friends. In his code, each letter of the alphabet is represented by a unique symbol. When asked how old he is, Vince writes:

+$@&#

Vince has an older brother. Vince is asked how many years younger than his brother he is. Vince writes:

#?=

How old is Vince's brother?

A 10
B 12
C 14
D 18

Answers and explanations on pages 81–84

1 Geoff, Hannah, Isaac, Jasmine and Leo compete in a basketball-shooting competition. They are the only competitors. They are awarded a place based on the number of shots they make.

Hannah makes more baskets than Isaac. Jasmine makes fewer baskets than Leo but more than Hannah.

If Geoff came third in the competition, who came fourth?

A Hannah

B Isaac

C Jasmine

D Leo

2 Yasi and Georgia play handball every day. They are both equally talented at the game and each win roughly the same number of games against each other.

Shona: I don't know how many games Yasi and Georgia played against each other this week but I know Georgia won ten so they must have played 20 games.

Which of the following statements shows the mistake Shona has made?

A Either Yasi or Georgia might have played unusually well this week.

B Yasi and Georgia have each won around half of the games but not exactly half.

C Yasi and Georgia may not have played 20 games this week.

D Yasi and Georgia may not have kept score in all of the games.

3 Colin wants Toni to help him wash the car on Thursday, Friday or Saturday but he won't wash the car if it's going to rain. The Bureau predicts that it might rain on Thursday and/or Friday and Toni is busy on Saturday so is unavailable to help on that day.

Which of the following is **not** possible?

A Toni offers to help Colin on Thursday.

B Colin could wash the car on Friday.

C It will rain on Thursday.

D Toni will help Colin on Saturday.

4 The following solid is part of a 3D puzzle.

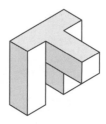

Which of the following solids will fit with the piece above to make a cube?

A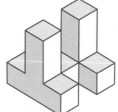

B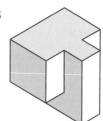

C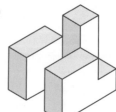

D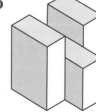

☞ Answers and explanations on pages 84–87

5 Mia arrived at the aged-care facility and saw the cleaner switch on the television in her grandmother's room.

A carer turns on the television for her grandmother every day except Saturdays and Sundays when the television either remains off or is turned on by the cleaner. The cleaner only works on Mondays, Wednesdays and Sundays in the mornings and every Friday afternoon. The cleaner is always fifteen minutes early on Mondays and Wednesdays.

Which of the following sentences must be correct?

A Today is Sunday.

B Today is either Monday or Wednesday.

C The carer is unexpectedly away.

D Today must be Friday.

6 Here are some square pieces of paper. They are labelled with numbers and some of them have holes cut out of them.

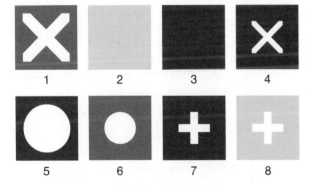

The following image was made by placing four of these pieces on top of each other in a particular order.

What is the order that the pieces were placed?

A 2, 6, 4, 5

B 3, 8, 1, 5

C 2, 7, 1, 5

D 2, 1, 8, 5

7 In the nation of Geldonia, there are four types of coin. There are 3 fingot in 1 glingot and 2 glingots in 1 hengol. If there are 30 fingots in 1 ingol, how many hengols are in 1 ingol?

A 5

B 6

C 20

D 45

8 Someone has removed one of the baobab trees from the newly planted roundabout near Lily's house. Whoever did it must have noticed it being planted and had a motive to take it and also an opportunity.

If this is true, which of the following must be true?

A If Lily had both an opportunity and a motive, she must have taken the tree.

B If Lily did not steal the tree, she cannot have had a motive.

C If Lily stole the tree, she cannot have had a motive.

D If Lily had a motive, she must have been the one to take the tree.

9 Lana said: 'It's a waste of time for the majority of students to study maths past the basic maths needed for Year 6 as most of us are never going to need complicated maths in our day-to-day lives or jobs.'

Which statement weakens Lana's argument?

A There is less benefit in studying maths now than at any time in history.

B Basic maths in useful in everyday life.

C Education institutions often require some level of maths for entry.

D Some teachers don't help students appreciate the relevance of maths.

10 The following string of shapes is part of a game.

A single move consists of a player tapping two consecutive shapes. The shapes that are tapped will change in the following way:

- A square will turn into a triangle.
- A triangle will turn into a circle.
- A circle will turn into a square.

Which of the following is it **not** possible to see inside the string after only one move?

A △○○△

B □○○□

C ○□○□

D □○□○

11 Malnutrition is caused by nutritional deficiencies. Left untreated, malnutrition has severe long-term impacts on children's physical and mental health. A cost-effective treatment for malnutrition is peanut paste. The paste is enriched with vitamins, minerals and protein powder to create a nutritious food supplement that is distributed by charity organisations to children at risk of malnutrition in areas of drought, war or natural disaster.

Which statement most strengthens the above argument?

A Peanut paste is stored in foil sachets.

B Peanut paste is cost effective to produce, store, transport and distribute.

C Children only need three peanut-paste sachets a day for six weeks to overcome malnutrition.

D People are urged to donate to charities which provide this lifesaving product where it's needed.

12 If Sharna can't get time off work at Christmas, then she won't be able to drive to Sydney with her work colleague, Evie, and share the driving.

If Sharna does get time off and she is a good driver of Evie's car, then she might convince Evie to go to Sydney at Easter too.

Evie won't be happy, though, if Sharna is a poor driver and Evie has announced that if so, it will be the last time she ever takes Sharna to Sydney by car.

Which one of the following outcomes is **not** possible?

A Sharna did not go to Sydney even though she got time off work.

B Sharna got time off work and, after the trip, Evie said she'd never drive to Sydney with Sharna again.

C Evie said she'd drive to Sydney with Sharna at Easter even though Sharna was a poor driver.

D Sharna did not get time off work for Christmas.

13 I have four cards. Each card has a letter printed on each side. No letter appears twice on the cards. The cards can be set out to show the four words below:

Which word below can also be spelt out using the cards?

A PAWN   B WASP

C SHIP   D SNOW

SAMPLE TEST 2A

14

> **Bella**: Aunty always says 'a stitch in time saves nine' when she wants me to keep my bedroom tidy.

If the information in the box is true, whose reasoning is correct?

A **Carly**: That proverb means you should not procrastinate or put things off because you'll worry for nine times longer.

B **Liev**: That proverb means you should sew up torn or ripped clothing immediately.

C **Phillipa**: That proverb means you should do things well the first time to save having to redo them later.

D **Braiden**: That proverb means you should fix a problem when it's small rather than wait until it likely becomes a bigger problem.

15 The following is the net of a six-sided dice.

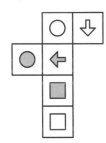

Which of the following is **not** a view of the dice?

A   B

C   D

16 Alyssa's school is offering an after-school course in engineering. As well as considering students' personal attributes, such as reliability and attitude to hard work, the school has also set a maths test and a thinking skills test.

If a student's personal attributes are suitable, then the student only needs to pass the thinking skills test to be accepted into the course.

If a student's personal attributes are not particularly strong, then they either need an outstanding thinking skills test score or to do well in both the maths test and the thinking skills test.

Alyssa has an interest in engineering and excellent personal attributes but failed to be accepted into the course.

What must have been the reason?

A She did not get an excellent result in the thinking skills test.

B She failed the maths test.

C She failed the thinking skills test.

D Her personal attributes were not outstanding.

17 Niall, Ish, Ethan and Regan are four friends. Each friend has a unique collection of stamps and coins.

■ The person with the most stamps also has the most coins.

■ Niall has more coins than Regan but fewer stamps.

■ Ish has fewer coins than Ethan and fewer stamps than Niall.

■ Niall has fewer coins than Ish.

Who has the fewest stamps?

A Niall

B Ish

C Ethan

D Regan

☞ Answers and explanations on pages 84–87

18 Hayley and Eddie have told their parents they might dye their hair pink for their end-of-year class party. Their parents have agreed as long as the children get good end-of-year reports from their teachers.

Nandita: 'Eddie dyed his hair pink for the party so he must have got a good end-of-year report.'

Kamal: 'Hailey didn't dye her hair pink. She mustn't have got a good end-of-year report.'

If the information in the box is true, whose reasoning is correct?

A Nandita only

B Kamal only

C Both Nandita and Kamal

D Neither Nandita nor Kamal

19 A rectangular room that measures 2.2 m by 2.7 m is covered by square carpet tiles that are 0.5 m along each side. If a full carpet tile is used in one corner, what are the dimensions of the tile that will be used in the opposite corner?

A 0.2 × 0.2 m

B 0.2 × 0.3 m

C 0.2 × 0.5 m

D 0.2 × 0.7 m

20 Willow the dog has a litter of five puppies: P, Q, R, S and T. Each pup's fur can be described by two things: a main colour and a pattern. The colours are white and grey. The patterns are spotted, flecked and saddle.

- P is white and has spots.
- Q is white and saddle.
- Two dogs are grey.
- Two dogs are flecked.

Given the information above, what **must** be true?

A There is at least one white flecked puppy.

B There are two spotted puppies.

C There is at least one grey saddled puppy.

D There is at least one grey flecked puppy.

1 Cameron, Desh, Emma, Finlay and Garth compete in a piano competition. They are the only competitors.

Finlay finished ahead of Emma. Garth finished two places behind Cameron.

If Finlay finished in third place, in which position did Desh finish?

A first

B second

C fourth

D fifth

2 The following solid is part of a 3D puzzle.

Which of the following solids will fit with the piece above to make a cube?

A 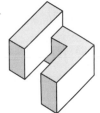   **B**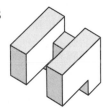

C 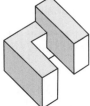   **D**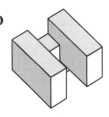

3 Mica said: '16 and 17-year-olds are mature enough to be allowed to vote. Prior to 1973 the voting age in Australia was 21. It was revised down to 18 in 1973 because it was deemed unfair that 18-year-olds were old enough to die as soldiers in wars yet not allowed to vote. The law should be revised again to allow people who are 16 and 17 to vote. Young people will inherit this planet so

16 and 17-year-olds should be allowed to vote for the politicians they think will make the best decisions for their future.'

Which one of these statements, if true, most weakens Mica's argument?

A 16 and 17-year-olds are easily influenced by others.

B Many 16 and 17-year-olds are not interested in politics.

C It should not be compulsory for 16 and 17-year-olds to vote because not all of them are politically engaged.

D Many 16 and 17-year-olds work and pay tax on their wages so it's unfair to take their tax but not let them vote.

4 In a cycling competition, cyclists can win medals for placing first, second or third. They can also win a medal for climbing the mountain the fastest. This medal is called the 'Top of the Mountain' medal.

Arabella: 'This means that after the race there will be four winners.'

Which one of the following sentences shows the mistake Arabella has made?

A More than one cyclist may receive a 'Best and Fairest' medal.

B The 'Top of the Mountain' medal can only be awarded when there is a mountain in the race.

C The 'Top of the Mountain' medal may have been won by a cyclist who placed first, second or third in the race.

D The skills of cyclists will vary so it's impossible to predict who will win the 'Top of the Mountain' medal.

5 Here are some square pieces of paper. They are labelled with numbers and some of them have holes cut out of them.

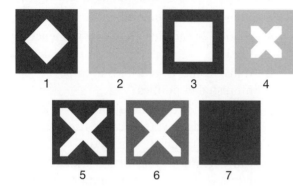

1 2 3 4

5 6 7

The following image was made by placing four of these pieces on top of each other in a particular order.

In which order were the pieces placed?

A 7, 4, 6, 3

B 2, 6, 1, 3

C 7, 1, 6, 3

D 2, 1, 6, 3

6 To become a successful chef you need time-management skills and a passion for food and cooking. You must be able to work under pressure and listen to and accept instructions.

Otto: 'Bianca has a passion for food and can follow instructions and is well-organised. She's certain to make a great chef.'

Nikita: 'Tariq loves cooking and eating and has excellent time-management skills but he doesn't always listen to instructions so he'll struggle working in a kitchen.'

If the information in the box is true, whose reasoning is correct?

A Otto only

B Nikita only

C Both Ottto and Nikita

D Neither Otto nor Nikita

7 Celia ordered a pizza delivery from her favourite restaurant. It was delivered at 8 pm but not by Celia's favourite driver, who works every day except Mondays and Tuesdays but only works from 11am until 5 pm on Wednesdays and 11am until 9 pm on Thursdays to Sundays. The restaurant does not deliver after 9 pm.

Which of the following sentences must be correct?

A Today is Sunday.

B Today is either Saturday or Sunday.

C Today must be Thursday.

D Today must be Wednesday.

8 In a game that uses plastic chips to represent points, there are red chips worth 3 points, purple chips worth 5 points and blue chips worth 10 points.

Bindi has three times as many purple chips as blue chips and five more red chips than blue chips.

If Bindi has a total of 20 coloured chips, how many points does she have?

A 63

B 80

C 99

D 129

9 A special deck of cards is made. On one side of each card is either a square, a cross or a circle. The reverse of each card is either left blank or has the same shape as on the other side.

Three of these cards are shown, dealt out in a row.

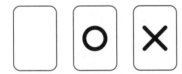

Gordon flips the first card over. He then flips the first two cards over. Finally he flips all three cards.

Which of the following is it possible for Gordon to see?

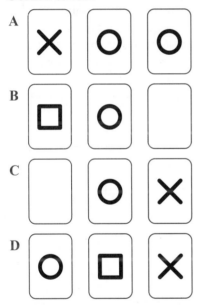

10 The swim carnival holds a series of heats before the semifinals and then the final in each event.

Every swimmer who places first, second or third in a heat competes in one of four semifinals. The best two swimmers in each semifinal then compete in the single final event.

Cameron: 'Jeremy was faster than Josef in their heat so if Josef qualifies for the semifinals, so will Jeremy.'

Which statement must be true?

A Josef would need to have come first, second or third in his heat for Cameron's statement to be true.

B Josef may not have swum as fast as the other swimmers in the heat.

C Josef would need to have come second or third in his heat for Cameron's statement to be true.

D Jeremy and Josef likely tied for first place.

11 The numbers 1 to 8 are written randomly on the front and back of four cards. Each card has one number on each side. Each card has a value that is the sum of the two numbers written on it. For example, a card that has a 1 on one side and a 2 on the other would have a value of 3.

Of the four cards, one card has a value of 9, one has a value of 10 and one has a value of 11.

If the 4 and 2 are not on the same card, what must be true?

A The 1 and 5 are on the same card.

B The 2 and 7 are on the same card.

C The 3 and 8 are on the same card.

D The 4 and 7 are on the same card.

12 Recent research has shown that it's the certainty of being caught rather than the severity of any penalty that deters people from committing crimes.

Which one of the following shows **incorrect** reasoning?

A **Rachel:** 'This shows that people are more likely to commit crimes if they think they won't get caught.'

B **Brooke:** 'This shows that larger fines won't have any impact on the number of crimes committed.'

C **Chris:** 'This shows that more police are needed to patrol the roads and deter people from wrongdoing.'

D **Oli:** 'This shows that not fining people or threatening them with jail helps to deter them from committing crimes.'

SAMPLE TEST 2B

13 The following is one view of a six-sided dice.

Which of the following is the only possible net of the dice?

A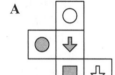

B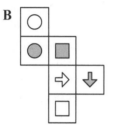

C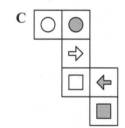

D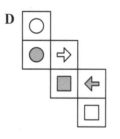

14 Ms Chen, the sports teacher, decided to investigate whether eating a cup of red jelly before a cross-country run made any difference to the time taken for her students to run the course.

She divided the class into two groups according to their birth months. Students born during odd months (January, March, May, July, September and November) were given a cup of red jelly before each cross-country run for six weeks. Students born in even months (February, April, June, August, October and December) were given green jelly before they ran for the six weeks of the investigation.

On average the students who were given red jelly ran the course faster over the six weeks than the students who ate the green jelly.

Ms Chen: 'So it's true that eating red jelly before a cross-country run helps students run the course at a faster pace.'

Which one of the following shows the mistake Ms Chen has made?

A Some students might have been eating red jelly at home too.

B The students who were given the red jelly may have been faster on average at cross country anyway.

C The students who were given green jelly may have performed better at mental tasks.

D More students may have been born in odd months than even months.

15 James, Amelia, Samuel and Lily are four friends. Each friend has a unique collection of rare comic books and action figures.

- The person who has the most comic books has the second-most action figures.
- The person who has the fewest comic books has the most action figures.
- James has more comic books than Amelia but fewer than Lily.
- Samuel doesn't have the most of anything, or the fewest.

Who has the fewest action figures?

A James

B Amelia

C Samuel

D Lily

16 Howard goes for a run every day between Town A and Town B along a straight road. He runs at a constant speed and it takes him 20 minutes. Lillian walks the same stretch of road in the opposite direction, leaving Town B and walking towards Town A. She walks at a constant speed and it takes her 60 minutes to complete the walk.

If they both leave at 10 am, what time will they pass each other?

A 10:05 am   **B** 10:10 am

C 10:12 am   **D** 10:15 am

17 Listening to music has a therapeutic effect on the brain. Music helps people recall pleasant memories and feelings, thereby enhancing mood and reducing anxiety. Individual sounds can also be used as a form of therapy. A cat's purr, for example, has been found to have therapeutic, relaxing effects and to improve heart health.

Which one of the following statements most strengthens the above argument?

A Music activates cognitive, motor and speech centres in the brain.

B Himalayan or crystal singing bowls, gongs and singing in one tone can be used in sound therapy.

C Music therapy can help cancer patients deal with anxiety and depression.

D Music therapy is useful in residential aged care.

18 A consumer research company conducted market research on mattresses.

Results showed that:

- The softest Dreamsleeper brand mattresses were softer than the softest Cosy-up Comfort range of mattresses.

- The Supersoft range of Horizon Air mattresses were softer than the softest Dreamsleeper mattresses.

- The softest Cosy-up Comfort mattresses were softer than the Horizon Cloud but not as soft as the softest Dreamsleeper.

- Dreamsleeper was more expensive than Cosy-up Comfort or Horizon Cloud and the most expensive mattress was the Horizon Air.

If the above information is true, whose reasoning is correct?

A **Ashley**: 'I want the softest mattress I can find but I can't afford the most expensive mattress so I'll choose the Horizon Air.'

B **Conrad**: 'I love soft mattresses but I don't want the softest as that would be too soft so I'll choose a Horizon Air.'

C **Nikky**: 'I want the softest mattress money can buy so I'll get a Dreamsleeper.'

D **Rowan**: 'I like a medium-soft mattress but I'm on a budget so I'll buy a Cosy-up Comfort.'

19 Eli's soccer club wants to organise an end-of-year party. Club members were surveyed to find out what type of party they would prefer. The survey found that everyone who liked the idea of a disco also liked a bowling party. Plus anyone who liked a bowling party also liked the idea of a beach party but no-one who liked the idea of a bowling party liked the idea of laser tag.

Based on the above information, which one of the following must be true?

A If Eli likes a disco party, he does not like a bowling party.

B If Hugo does not like laser tag, he does not like a beach party.

C If Ava likes a disco, she does not like laser tag.

D If Clara likes a beach party, she also likes a bowling party.

20 Prue sends messages to her friends in code. The code is always the same and uses a unique symbol to represent each letter of the alphabet; for example, Prue is &^#@.

When asked to name her favourite music genre, she wrote: $?+=

If she wrote one of the following genres, which one was it?

A rock

B jazz

C soul

D folk

1 Isabella, Gabriel, Mia, Oscar and Sandy are the only five competitors in a public-speaking competition.

Gabriel finished two places behind Mia.

Isabella finished ahead of Mia.

If Oscar finished in second place, in which place did Sandy finish?

A first

B third

C fourth

D fifth

2 Mr Brown coaches the debating team at Chloe and Jarrah's school. Every Wednesday there is a competition with other local schools. Mr Brown gets very excited whenever his team wins. But whenever they lose, he always gives homework the next day.

Chloe and Jarrah are walking home from school.

Chloe: 'Mr Brown definitely gave us homework last Thursday so the debating team must have lost last Wednesday.'

Jarrah: 'Today is Thursday and he didn't give us homework so the debating team must have won yesterday's competition.'

If the information in the box is true, whose reasoning is correct?

A Chloe only

B Jarrah only

C Both Chloe and Jarrah

D Neither Chloe nor Jarrah

3 If we don't all come to band practice this afternoon, Ms Webster will cancel the trip to the music festival next week.

If the trip to the festival goes ahead and it is successful, we might be able to convince Ms Webster to let us have a trip to the theme park at the end of term. But it won't be a success if the whole band doesn't learn the new piece.

If the festival trip is not successful, it will be the last trip Ms Webster will let us have.

If the above information is correct, which one of the following is **not** possible?

A The festival trip was cancelled even though everyone came to band practice that afternoon.

B The festival trip did not go ahead even though the whole class learned the new piece.

C The whole band learned the new piece but the festival trip was not a success.

D The whole band did not learn the new piece but Ms Webster let them go to the theme park at the end of term.

4 The following solid is part of a 3D puzzle.

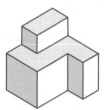

Which of the following solids will fit with the piece above to make a cube?

A 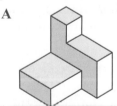   B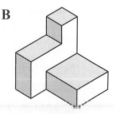

C 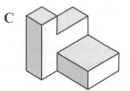   D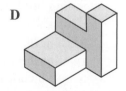

5 Ice forms when liquid water freezes but ice can take many different forms and shapes. You would have heard of icicles but you may not have heard of brinicles. A brinicle is a brine icicle that projects downwards from the ocean surface to the ocean floor. When seawater freezes, it releases its salt. This forms a salty brine. Brine is heavier than sea water so it sinks. As it sinks, the super-cold brine freezes any water it touches, forming a sinking spear all the way to the ocean floor. A web of ice then spreads across the ocean floor, freezing and killing anything it touches! That's why some people call a brinicle the 'finger of death'.

Which statement best expresses the main idea of the text?

A Ice forms when liquid water freezes and can take different shapes.

B A brinicle is an underwater icicle sometimes called a 'finger of death'.

C Not many people have heard of brinicles.

D As super-cold brine sinks, it freezes any water it touches.

6 Leo says: 'Reading a funny book is my favourite weekend activity. I can forget about homework, get lost in another world and have a good laugh!'

Which argument below uses the same structure as the above argument?

A Elaine: 'I don't like funny books. They are usually very silly.'

B Lina: 'I love playing the trumpet. It's great that I get to play in the school band, take private lessons and also practise on my own.'

C Ari: Ms Simon gives us really interesting projects and it's fun thinking about interesting ways to present them. So I like doing homework.'

D Ethan: 'Graphic novels are the best. The library has some new graphic novels that are really funny.'

7 Here are some square pieces of paper. They are labelled with numbers and some of them have holes cut out of them.

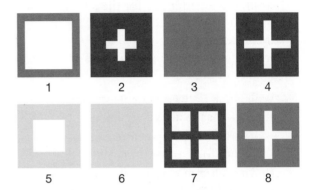

The following image was made by placing four of these pieces on top of each other in a particular order.

In which order were the pieces placed?

A 3, 5, 4, 1

B 5, 3, 7, 1

C 8, 2, 5, 1

D 6, 2, 4, 7

8 Virat made some money running a car wash in his front yard. At the end of the day he counted the notes he had earned.

He had twice as many $20 notes as $10 notes. He had three times as many $5 notes as $50 notes.

If Virat had a total of $345, how many $5 notes did he have?

A 3

B 6

C 9

D 15

9 The local council announced that a new bike park would be constructed at the site of the old shopping centre. The council said this would be a better use for the site than the previous plan to build a botanical garden there because the bike park would specifically cater to young children new to mountain biking.

Which one of these statements, if true, most strengthens the above argument?

A The old shopping centre site has been vacant for the last three years.

B There is a mountain-bike park and trail suitable for all levels in the next suburb.

C There are no public gardens or open spaces within a 20-km radius of the site.

D A survey found that young children new to mountain biking are not catered for in the area.

10 The following string of shapes is part of a game.

A single move consists of a player tapping two consecutive shapes. The shapes that are tapped will change in the following way:

■ A square will turn into a triangle.
■ A triangle will turn into a circle.
■ A circle will turn into a square.

Which of the following is it **not** possible to see inside the string after only one move?

11 Oliver and Yitong are cutting out designs for an art project. Yitong is left-handed.

Oliver: 'We'd better hurry up. We need to get these finished before the bell goes.'

Yitong: 'My hand is aching. These right-handed scissors are so uncomfortable and difficult for left-handed people to use. The government should give a subsidy so that left-handed people can buy left-handed scissors.'

Which one of these statements, if true, most weakens Yitong's argument?

A There may be higher-priority issues that need financial support from the government.

B Oliver and Yitong still have a lot to do and they need to finish before the bell goes.

C Left-handed people often have to pay more for specialised tools.

D Using right-handed scissors can be painful for left-handed people.

12 Ms Chan said: 'Whoever was selected as player of the match must have had a big impact on the game and must have shown a positive attitude.'

If what Ms Chan said is true, which one of these conclusions must also be true?

A If Dora did not have a big impact on the game, she cannot have been selected as player of the match.

B If Hebe had a big impact on the game and showed a positive attitude, she must have been selected as player of the match.

C If Adam did not have a big impact on the game, he must not have shown a positive attitude.

D If Ezra was not selected as player of the match, he must not have shown a positive attitude.

13 I have four cards. Each card has a letter printed on each side. No letter appears twice on the cards. The cards can be set out to show the four words below:

Which word below **cannot** also be spelt out using the cards?

A PEAT

B PAST

C BANK

D TAPE

14 The following is the net of a six-sided dice.

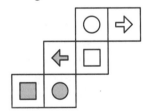

Which of the following is **not** a view of the dice?

A 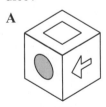   B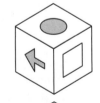

C   D

15 Eastside Public School has a zero-tolerance policy towards littering in the playground. Every recess and lunchtime, an extra teacher is rostered on playground duty as 'litter guard'. The sole job of the litter guard is to patrol the playground and catch any student littering instead of using the rubbish, composting or recycling bins. Any student caught littering gets lunchtime detention for a full month.

In the last two terms, not a single student has been caught littering and the playground has been litter free. Today Mr White is rostered to be litter guard.

Mr White: 'The fact that litter guards never catch anyone littering proves that being a litter guard is a waste of time! Teachers should be able to use their time to do something more useful, such as preparing lessons!'

Which one of the following statements shows the mistake Mr White has made?

A Just because the litter guards have not caught anyone does not mean no students have littered.

B The teacher already rostered to playground duty could also watch for any students littering.

C Fear of being caught and lunchtime detention might be the reason why students don't litter.

D The teachers at Eastside Public School already have some extra time to prepare lessons.

SAMPLE TEST 3A

16 Kala saw a leaflet on the noticeboard at the local shopping centre. The leaflet advertised a new pet store. The advertisement claimed:

'If you buy pet fish in a bowl, you won't want to look at a screen so often! So buy a fish today!'

Which assumption has the writer of the leaflet made to draw the conclusion in the advertisement?

A There is a new pet store at the shopping centre.

B People should buy a pet fish in a bowl.

C Not looking at screens so often is a good thing.

D If you have a pet fish, you won't want to look at a screen so often.

17 Aiden, Kimberley, Daphne and Scarlett are four friends participating in a science fair. They are judged on how interesting their experiment is and on their written report.

■ The person who had the least interesting experiment also had the worst report.

■ The person who had the third-best report had the most interesting experiment.

■ Aiden's experiment was deemed more interesting than Daphne's but less interesting than Scarlett's.

If Aiden had the second-most interesting experiment, whose report was third best?

A Aiden

B Kimberley

C Daphne

D Scarlett

18 Numbers are in decline for many of our native wildlife species but there are things you can do at home to help them stay safe. One simple thing you can do is provide water. Put fresh water in a shallow dish in a shady spot on the ground. This can be lifesaving to wildlife on hot days. Another easy thing you can do is keep your pets indoors at night so that nocturnal birds and animals stay safe.

Also don't use rat poison and slug bait that build up in the food chain and unintentionally kill native wildlife.

Which statement best expresses the main idea of the text?

A Numbers are in decline for many of our native wildlife species.

B Each pet cat kills on average 110 native animals per year.

C There are things you can do at home to help native wildlife stay safe.

D Rat poison and slug bait can unintentionally kill native wildlife.

19 A 1-m^2 garden-bed kit that is made up of four 1-m sides can be attached to other kits to create garden beds of different areas. If I have one kit already, what is the minimum number of kits I must buy to increase the area of the garden bed to 4 m^2?

A 1

B 2

C 3

D 4

20 A, B, C, D and E are five language students. Each student lives in either Australia or the United Kingdom. Each student is learning two of the following four languages: French, German, Mandarin or Japanese.

■ A is learning German and Mandarin.

■ B is learning Mandarin and Japanese.

■ C lives in Australia and is learning Japanese.

■ The same number of people are learning French and Mandarin.

■ E lives in the UK and is learning Japanese.

■ No-one who lives in Australia is learning French.

What must be true?

A Exactly 3 people are learning German.

B Exactly 3 people are learning Japanese.

C Exactly 2 people are learning German.

D Exactly 2 people are learning French.

☞ **Answers and explanations on pages 90–93**

1 Aria, Julian, Lim, Sonny and Tom are the only five competitors in a speed-climbing competition. The aim is to climb the rock wall as fast as possible.

Tom beat Lim.

Julian finished three places ahead of Aria.

If Sonny came fourth, where did Lim finish?

A first

B second

C third

D fifth

2 The following solid is part of a 3D puzzle.

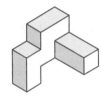

Which of the following solids will fit with the piece above to make a cube?

A

B
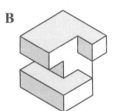

C
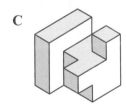

D
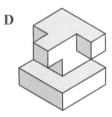

3
Spiders are often disliked and even feared by many people. However, since spiders are natural predators of insects they play an important role in controlling insect populations and maintaining the balance in an ecosystem.

Ruby: 'My dad is really fussy about everything outside being neat and tidy. As soon as he sees a spider web, he always brushes it away. Maybe that's why we have so many flies at our house!'

Alex: 'My mum is the same. That must be why we have a fly problem too.'

If the information in the box is true, whose reasoning is correct?

A Ruby only

B Alex only

C Both Ruby and Alex

D Neither Ruby nor Alex

4 People should be allowed to take their dog to work. Research shows that having a dog in the workplace reduces the stress levels of workers and also makes them more productive.

Which argument below uses the same structure as the above argument?

A Dogs are the best! They help build a sense of community. Bring your dog to work!

B Some people are allergic to dogs or afraid of dogs. So allowing dogs at work will limit job opportunities for some people.

C Dogs are a nuisance. From my experience they bark excessively and destroy property.

D People should not be allowed to take their dog to work. If the dog injures someone, there could be costly legal fees, compensation claims and damage to the company's reputation.

5 Here are some square pieces of paper. They are labelled with numbers and some of them have holes cut out of them.

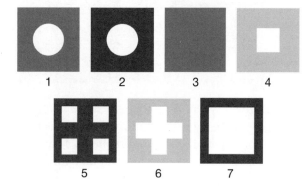

1 2 3 4

5 6 7

The following image was made by placing four of these pieces on top of each other in a particular order.

What is the order in which the pieces were placed?

A 3, 4, 6, 3   B 1, 6, 5, 7
C 5, 3, 2, 6   D 3, 2, 6, 7

6 Kaylee and her friends have been talking about having an end-of-term party. They want to have it at the beach but in the night-time with a bonfire. Kaylee wants to go but her parents won't let her. They say she is too young to go to the beach at night.

Kaylee: 'There's nothing wrong with going to a beach party at night. All my friends are going!'

Which assumption has Kaylee made to draw her conclusion?

A There's nothing wrong with going to a beach party at night.

B It's okay to do something if all your friends are doing it.

C All Kaylee's friends are going to the night-time beach party.

D Kaylee is not allowed to go to the beach at night.

7 Connie sold bags of homemade biscuits at a market stall one Sunday. She sold bags of either 3, 5 or 8 biscuits. At the end of the day, she had a number of bags left over.

She had three times as many bags with 8 biscuits as bags with 5 biscuits.

If there were 90 biscuits left over, how many bags of 3 biscuits did she fail to sell?

A 1   B 3   C 6   D 10

8 A special deck of cards is made. On one side of each card is either a square, a cross or a circle. The reverse of each card is either left blank or has the same shape as on the other side.

Three of these cards are shown, dealt out in a row.

Jin flips the first card over. He then flips the first two cards over. Finally he flips all three cards.

Which of the following is it **not** possible for Jin to see?

A

B

C

D

☞ Answers and explanations on pages 93–96

9 Amanda's music teacher told the class: 'To have even a chance of winning a prize in the end-of-year eisteddfod, you must have practised for at least 20 minutes at least five times a week.'

If Amanda's teacher is correct, which one of these statements must be true?

A All the students who practise for 20 minutes five times a week will win a prize.

B Only the students who practise for 20 minutes five times a week will win a prize.

C Some of the students who practise for less than 20 minutes each night will win a prize.

D None of the students who practise for less than 20 minutes five times a week will win a prize.

10 Space debris or junk refers to objects, such as paint flecks, screws, old satellites or even rocket stages, that are no longer useful but still in orbit around the Earth. It can pose a serious threat to the safety of satellites and other spacecraft in orbit and is an ongoing concern for space agencies and governments around the world. It is an international problem so an international fund should be established to deal with it.

Which one of these statements, if true, most strengthens the above argument?

A Space debris can have environmental impacts as it falls back to Earth.

B Each country has a responsibility to manage its own space junk.

C Finance is needed for international research into the environmental impacts of space debris.

D A fund might encourage some space technology companies to shirk their responsibilities.

11 The numbers 1 to 8 are written randomly on the front and back of four cards. Each card has one number on each side. Each card has a value that is the sum of the two numbers written on it. For example, a card that has a

1 on one side and a 2 on the other would have a value of 3.

Of the four cards, two have a value of 8 and one has a value of 5.

The four cards are arranged to show a four-digit number. Which of the following is the only possible arrangement?

A 1 2 4 5

B 1 2 5 7

C 2 3 5 7

D 2 3 6 8

12 Bella's school has a robotics team which Bella wants to join. To qualify to join the robotics team, a student must have attended a weekend introduction to robotics workshop.

Ivy: 'Bella wanted to join the team last term but hasn't attended the introduction to robotics workshop yet. I know she went to the workshop on the weekend. So she will definitely be chosen to be in the robotics team this term.'

Which one of the following sentences shows the mistake Ivy has made?

A After the workshop, Ivy might have decided she is not interested in robotics.

B There might not be enough equipment available for the robotics team this term.

C Fewer students applied to be in the robotics team this term.

D Attending the workshop might not be the only criterion used to select team members.

13 The following is one view of a six-sided dice.

Which of the following is the only possible net of the dice?

A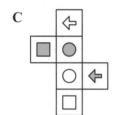

B

C

D

14 Daniel, Eduardo, Garant and Ming participated in a singing talent show. There were no other competitors. Competitors were ordered by the judges' scores based on stage presence and voice.

■ The person who had the best stage presence had the second-best voice.

■ The person who had the worst stage presence had the best voice.

■ Garant was ranked neither the best nor worst in either category.

If Ming had the second-best stage presence, where did she rank in vocal ability?

A first

B second

C third

D fourth

15 Braith begins walking a trail loop at 7 am. The loop starts and ends at the same place. He walks at a constant speed and arrives back at 12 noon.

Colleen rides her bike on the same loop but she goes in the opposite direction. She leaves at 7 am and arrives back at 8:15 am.

If they both travelled at a constant speed and made no stops, at what time did they pass each other?

A 7:15 am   B 7:45 am

C 7:48 am   D 8 am

16

Luna: 'Let's go to the cinema tonight. It's the opening night of that new movie you really want to see!'

Carlos: 'I'd better not. I have to iron my clothes and then get an early night or I'll likely look a mess and be tired for my job interview tomorrow. I really want the job. And if I'm tired and look a mess, I won't make a good impression.'

Luna: 'If you make a good impression, you might be offered the job. Otherwise you don't stand a chance! Let's go to the movies tomorrow night instead and celebrate your interview being over!

Based on the above information, which one of the following **cannot** be true?

A Carlos went to the movies with Luna but was offered the job.

B Carlos was tired and looked a mess at the interview but was offered the job.

C Carlos made a good impression but was not offered the job.

D Carlos did not go to the movies with Luna and was not offered the job.

17 Livvy is having a party tonight. Alice and Emily are sisters. They want to go to Livvy's party but their parents have said that anyone who has not tidied their own bedroom will not be allowed to go.

Livvy: 'Emily is not coming to the party but Alice is. Alice must have tidied her room.'

Dylan: 'And Emily must not have tided *her* room.'

If the information in the box is true, whose reasoning is correct?

A Livvy only

B Dylan only

C Both Livvy and Dylan

D Neither Livvy nor Dylan

18 Forest West Sports Club wants to build a wavepool in the club grounds. Approval from the local council is needed before construction can begin.

The owner of Forest West Sports Club claims: 'Our wavepool will make use of the latest technology to create a variety of different surf waves at the touch of a button. If we are granted approval to go ahead with construction, it will benefit the whole town of Forest West. It will give our young people a previously undreamed-of opportunity to surf—with not a beach in sight!

Which one of these statements, if true, most weakens the owner's argument?

A Forest West is a large town and a three-hour drive from the nearest beach.

B The technology behind the wavepool can create a wave every 8 to 10 seconds.

C Forest West has an old swimming pool owned and operated by the local council.

D Forest West Sports Club is an exclusive 'members only' facility.

19 George and Violet are out with their little brother Ben.

George: 'If we buy hot chips, it will encourage Ben to eat junk food.'

Violet: 'We'd better not buy hot chips!'

Which assumption has Violet made to draw her conclusion?

A There is a shop nearby that sells hot chips.

B George and Violet must not buy hot chips.

C George and Violet must not encourage Ben to eat junk food.

D If George and Violet buy hot chips, it will encourage Ben to eat junk food.

20 T, U, V, W and X are five musicians. Each musician has either brown or blue eyes. Each musician plays two of the four following instruments: guitar, piano, drums and saxophone.

- V plays piano and drums.
- W plays the guitar and has blue eyes.
- Only one person doesn't play the piano and they have brown eyes.
- Two people play the saxophone.
- More people play the guitar than the drums.

If the information is all that is provided, which of the following is the only possible statement?

A T and U play the same instruments.

B T and V play the same instruments.

C T and W play the same instruments.

D T and X play the same instruments.

THINKING SKILLS TEST | YEAR 6

SAMPLE TEST 4A

20 MIN

1 Sandrine, Violet, Lucas, Billa and Ryder are the only five competitors in a maths competition. The competitors are ordered on how many questions they complete correctly.

Billa completed fewer questions correctly than Violet.

Sandrine completed more questions than Ryder but fewer than Billa.

If Ryder came fourth, in what position did Lucas come?

A first

B second

C third

D fifth

2 Anh's school was selecting students to attend the filming of the school band performing on a breakfast television program. As well as considering students' previous interest in filmmaking, the school set students a public-speaking challenge and a music test.

If a student had a record of previous interest in filmmaking, then they only had to pass the public-speaking challenge to be selected to attend. If a student did not have a record of previous interest in filmmaking, then they either needed an excellent result in the public-speaking challenge or they needed to do well in both the public-speaking challenge and the music test.

Anh was in the film club so he had a good record of previous interest in filmmaking but failed to be selected to attend the filming of the program. What must have been the reason?

A Anh did badly in the music test.

B Anh failed the public-speaking challenge.

C Anh did not have a record of previous interest in filmmaking.

D Anh did well in the public-speaking challenge but badly in the music test.

3 Labrador dogs tend to weigh more than other breeds.

Aida: 'We just took our dog to the vet to weigh him. He weighs 30 kilos!'

Jackson: 'Wow! That's a lot. Is your dog a Labrador?'

Aida: 'No.'

Jackson: 'My dog is. So she must weigh over 30 kilos!'

Aida: 'No, that's not right. My dog might weigh more than your dog.'

If the information in the box is true, whose reasoning is correct?

A Aida only

B Jackson only

C Both Aida and Jackson

D Neither Aida nor Jackson

4 The following solid is part of a 3D puzzle.

Which of the following solids will fit with the piece above to make a cube?

A 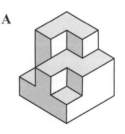   B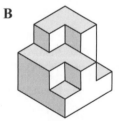

C 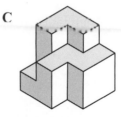   D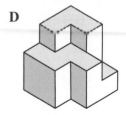

☞ Answers and explanations on pages 97–100

5 The student committee at Felicity's school wants to convince the principal to allow students to bring their pets into the classroom. Felicity is meeting the principal to make the case for the committee.

Felicity: 'Having our pets in the classroom will have a positive influence on students.'

Which one of these statements, if true, most weakens Felicity's argument?

A Pets can teach life skills such as patience and kindness.

B Pets can be an exciting distraction.

C Pets can be expensive to care for.

D Pets can provide comfort if a student is feeling anxious.

6 Here are some square pieces of paper. They are labelled with numbers and some of them have holes cut out of them.

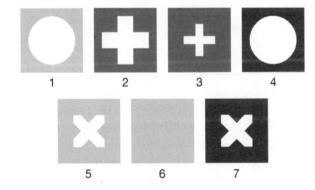

The following image was made by placing four of these pieces on top of each other in a particular order.

In which order were the pieces placed?

A 3, 5, 4, 1

B 6, 7, 2, 1

C 6, 2, 7, 1

D 6, 3, 7, 1

7 Each week Blake puts all his leftover silver coins into his piggy bank. At the end of the week, he takes what he has to the bank.

This week Blake found he had some of all four types of silver coins in his piggy bank. He had the same number of 10c coins as 50c coins and the same number of 5c coins as 20c coins.

If Blake has $3.75 in total, how many individual coins does he have?

A 12   **B** 16   **C** 24   **D** 30

8

Daisy's teacher said: 'There are two ways to qualify for the Regional Chess Tournament: by winning a local chess competition during the year or by accumulating a high-enough score total.'

This year seven students from Daisy's school qualified for the Regional Chess Tournament.

Daisy: 'I know that four local chess competitions were won by students from our school during the year. This means more than half our qualifiers for the Chess Tournament must be competition winners.'

Which one of the following sentences shows the mistake Daisy has made?

A Just because someone qualified for the Regional Chess Tournament, it doesn't mean they want to compete.

B The number of local chess competitions during the year may be higher this year.

C Some of the qualifiers for the Regional Chess Tournament may have won more than one local competition during the year.

D Some students may have missed some local competitions during the year.

9 **Garry:** 'Did you hear they are going to install shark nets at Cove beach?'

Talia: 'Oh no! Shark nets are not an effective way to protect swimmers. They are only 150 metres long and don't prevent sharks from swimming around them to enter the beach. They only operate by entangling any creature that swims into them by chance. Which means they kill dolphins, whales, sea turtles and other marine creatures, including critically endangered ones.'

Which one of these statements, if true, most strengthens Talia's argument?

A Scientists are developing shark-net alternatives that do not kill marine creatures.

B Forty per cent of sharks are caught in the nets on their way back out from the beach.

C Cove Beach is a popular tourist beach.

D Some shark nets are 160 metres long.

10 A special deck of cards is made. On one side of each card is either a square, a cross or a circle. The reverse of each card is either left blank or has the same shape as on the other side.

Four of these cards are shown, dealt out in a row.

If all the cards are then turned over, which of the following is the only possible view of them now?

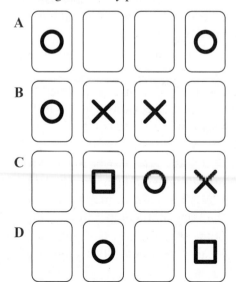

11 The 'Rock Fishing Safety Program' saves lives. The workshop sessions include reviewing and wearing correct lifejackets and also highlight hazards to avoid. Book your spot in a workshop today!

Which argument below uses the same structure as the above argument?

A The 'Rock Fishing Safety Program' is fantastic. Everyone attending a workshop gets a free lifejacket.

B The new Southside masterplan is underpinned by rigorous studies and includes changes which address all the feedback Council received during the public consultation phase. It will guarantee our town's future.

C Hilltown is set to become greener! The new 'Greening our City' program includes removing weed species that have taken over local parks and the planting of 6000 native trees and shrubs.

D The proposed boardwalk extension will destroy important natural habitat. The area to be cleared is environmentally sensitive. It also includes an endangered coastal orchard. Sign the petition to stop the boardwalk.

12 Stella feels strongly about environmental issues. She wrote a letter to the Environment Minister. This is what she wrote:

A krill is a tiny crustacean but krill populations are at the centre of the whole Antarctic marine-food web. This means they have an enormous impact on the health of our Southern Ocean and therefore the global oceans. Krill populations need our protection. They face threats from concentrated fishing and a warming planet. Threats to krill populations are threats to the planet. We must act to protect these vital krill populations.

Which statement best expresses the main idea in Stella's letter?

A A krill is a tiny crustacean.

B The biomass of Antarctic krill is around 380 million tonnes.

C Krill populations face threats from concentrated fishing and a warming planet.

D We must act to protect vital krill populations.

SAMPLE TEST 4A

13 Six friends are sitting in a circle facing inwards. Their names are Ash, Bongo, Candice, Desh, Elliot and Fernand. They are sitting in alphabetical order. They play a game that will result in two winners.

Ash starts. He gets up, walks clockwise around the circle, skipping Bongo and taking the seat of Candice. Candice is now out and there are only five people left around the circle. The next person to have a go is Desh because he is now the person sitting next, in a clockwise direction, to Ash. Desh gets up, skips the person next to him and eliminates the one after that by taking their seat.

If this process continues until there are only two people left, who are they?

A Ash and Desh   **B** Bongo and Elliot

C Ash and Bongo   **D** Elliot and Desh

14 Grace, Evie and Lily all collect toys to hang on their backpacks. Grace has dinosaurs, ponies, unicorns, sea animals and Australian animals. Evie has cartoon characters, Australian animals and sea animals. Lily has ponies, birds, sea animals, dogs and Australian animals.

What toys does Grace have that neither Evie nor Lily has?

A dogs and cartoon characters

B ponies and dinosaurs

C unicorns and sea creatures

D dinosaurs and unicorns

15 Will's teacher told the class there were three distinct components to the mark they each received for their project. She said each student received a mark for research, analysis and presentation.

- No-one passed all three components.
- No-one failed all three components.
- Everyone who passed analysis also passed one of the other two components.
- No-one who passed research failed the presentation.

Based on the above information, which one of the following **cannot** be true?

A Will passed both the analysis and research components.

B Will failed both the analysis and research components.

C Will passed only the presentation component.

D Will passed both the analysis and presentation components.

16 The following is the net of a six-sided dice.

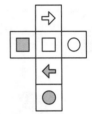

Which of the following is a view of the dice?

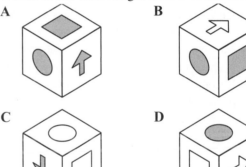

A   B

C   D

17 Virginia, Winnie, Yang and Zan are four friends participating in a pottery competition. There are no other competitors in their age group. They receive a rank for how many egg cups they can make in the given time and are also given a score based on how well the egg cups are made.

Virginia made fewer egg cups than Zan but scored higher than Yang.

Winnie made more egg cups than Yang and scored higher than Zan.

Zan made fewer egg cups than Yang but scored higher than Virginia.

For the person who made the worst egg cups, where did they rank in terms of quantity made?

A first   **B** second   **C** third   **D** fourth

18 Beekeepers are also known as apiarists. They manage beehives and the production of honey and related products. To be a successful beekeeper you need to enjoy plants and insects including bees. You also need to be happy to work alone and must have patience and a calm nature, as well as attention to detail when keeping records.

Carlos: 'Kyle always prefers working alone rather than in a group and when we go bushwalking he can name all the plants and insects we see. Plus he's so calm when we have to read to the Kindy classes. He's much more patient than me! He'd be a successful beekeeper for sure.'

Ashlee: 'Loren loves nature! She's happy to work in a group but she told me she really prefers to work alone. She keeps the records for our chess club. Mr Lin says she is brilliant at it! But I think she is scared of bees so beekeeper is definitely not for her.'

If the information in the box is true, whose reasoning is correct?

A Carlos only

B Ashlee only

C Both Carlos and Ashlee

D Neither Carlos nor Ashlee

19 It takes Gabby 45 minutes to lay down tiles that cover a rectangular area measuring 4 m by 9 m. How long will it take her to lay tiles over a rectangular area that measures 3 m by 8 m?

A 24 minutes

B 30 minutes

C 36 minutes

D 42 minutes

20 The main street of a country town includes five buildings in a row.

- The bakery, which is only one storey high, is next to the bank.
- The hardware store is three storeys high and is in the middle of the row.
- The music store is immediately to the left of the hardware store.
- The newsagent has twice as many storeys as the music store.
- The bank and the newsagent are equal in height.
- The bakery is separated from the music store by two other stores.

Which of the following correctly shows the street?

A

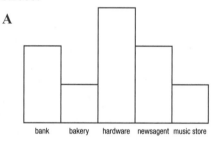

B

C

D

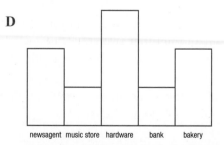

SAMPLE TEST 4B

20 MIN

1 Bodhi, Cai, Elio, Freya and Inara are the only five competitors in a go-cart race.

Cai beat Bodhi but finished after Inara.

Elio finished two places ahead of Cai.

Given this information it is not possible to work out where Freya finished. What is the only position in which Freya definitely did **not** finish?

A second

B third

C fourth

D fifth

2 The following solid is part of a 3D puzzle.

Which of the following solids will fit with the piece above to make a cube?

A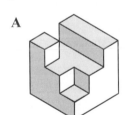

B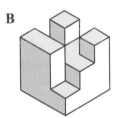

C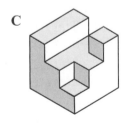

D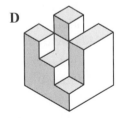

3 City West school is going to increase recess time as of next term. The principal says increasing recess time will be good for students' health and wellbeing, which in turn will be good for their academic performance. Studies have shown that physical activity can improve concentration, focus and memory retention.

Which one of these statements, if true, most strengthens the principal's argument?

A Increasing recess time is good for students' health and wellbeing.

B The increased recess time will require additional supervision and staffing.

C City West has a new playground under construction, due for completion next term.

D Recess provides opportunities for students to develop social skills and reduce anxiety.

4 People should smile more often. A new study, led by Stanford university, has found that arranging our facial muscles in a smile leads to an increase in happiness.

Which argument below uses the same structure as the argument in the box?

A 'The Big Smile' has spectacular special effects and an amazing soundtrack. It should have won the award for best movie.

B Our holiday last Christmas was the best. It made me so happy to see Gran. Let's go again.

C Seeking happiness through external factors is not a path to long-term happiness. External factors, such as money or fame, bring only temporary pleasure.

D The Black Creek Carnival is a must-see event. It is a celebration of Australian culture and has experiences to make the whole family happy.

5 A motel has 12 different rooms. Double rooms can sleep a maximum of two people. Triple rooms can sleep three people and family rooms can sleep five. The motel has the same number of triple rooms as family rooms.

One night the motel was at its maximum capacity of 36 people. How many double rooms does the motel have?

A 2

B 4

C 6

D 8

6 Here are some square pieces of paper. They are labelled with numbers and some of them have holes cut out of them.

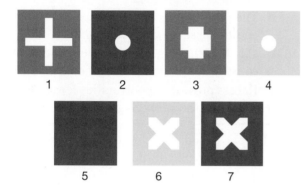

The following image was made by placing four of these pieces on top of each other in a particular order.

What is the order in which the pieces were placed?

A 5, 3, 2, 7   **B** 5, 4, 3, 7
C 5, 1, 6, 7   **D** 5, 3, 4, 7

7 Five applicants for a job were given a typing test. They had to type a passage as quickly as possible while also making sure they made no mistakes.

- Kimberley was slower than Sara but Sara was slower than Terry.
- Terry was faster than Monti but made three mistakes.
- Anjar made no mistakes but took the longest.
- Monti made fewer mistakes than Sara but finished after her.
- Sara finished second but made two mistakes.

If the above information is true, which one of the sentences below **cannot** be true?

A Monti made more mistakes than Anjar.
B Terry was not the first to finish the test.
C Terry was faster than Kimberley.
D Terry made the most mistakes.

8 There is far too much military spending. When governments spend money on the military, there is less to spend on addressing social or humanitarian issues such as healthcare, education and unemployment. It would be better to fund important progams in these areas.

Which one of these statements, if true, most weakens the above argument?

A Military spending can create jobs.
B Military research has led to advances in aviation technology.
C Governments worldwide are increasing levels of military spending.
D Poverty, hunger and disease affect millions of people around the world.

9
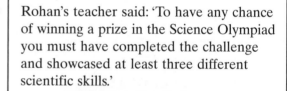
Rohan's teacher said: 'To have any chance of winning a prize in the Science Olympiad you must have completed the challenge and showcased at least three different scientific skills.'

Rohan: 'I completed the challenge and I showcased four different scientific skills. I'll win a prize for sure!'

Which one of the following sentences shows the mistake Rohan has made?

A The Science Olympiad tests students' knowledge and skills in science, technology, engineering and maths.
B Doing the minimum required to win a prize does not guarantee a prize.
C Some students were disqualified for using AI during the challenge.
D Some students completed the challenge in record time.

10 The numbers 1 to 10 are written randomly on the front and back of five cards. Each card has one number on each side. Each card has a value that is the sum of the two numbers written on it. For example, a card that has a 1 on one side and a 2 on the other would have a value of 3.

Of the five cards, two cards have a value of 14 and two cards have a value of 10.

Which statement must be true?

A The 9 and 5 are on the same card.

B The 6 and 8 are on the same card.

C The 4 and 10 are on the same card.

D The 1 and 9 are on the same card.

11 The Bridgetown local council made the following announcement in its newsletter:

A new Farmers' Market will be trialled next Saturday at Waratah Park. This location was chosen due to its popularity with families and its easy and safe access for walkers and cyclists. It is hoped the Farmers' Market will be a popular attraction in the area and become a regular event.

Which statement best expresses the main idea of the announcement?

A A Farmers' Market will be held next Saturday at Waratah Park.

B Waratah Park has easy and safe access.

C The Bridgetown local council voted in favour of the market at their last meeting.

D The Farmers' Market might become a regular event.

12 The following is the net of a six-sided dice.

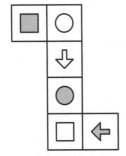

Which of the following is a view of the dice?

A 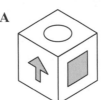 **B**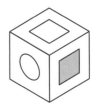

C 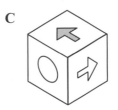 **D**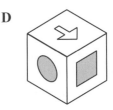

13 Nathan, Victoria, William and Zoe are four teammates participating in a basketball tournament. They can be ordered by the average number of points they scored per game and by their average number of assists.

■ The person with the most assists per game scored the fewest points per game.

■ The person with the fewest assists scored the third-highest number of points per game.

■ Nathan scored more points per game than Zoe, who was second for assists per game.

If the four players were ranked from first to fourth for assists, where would Nathan come?

A first

B second

C third

D fourth

14 It takes Pamela one hour to paint the ceiling in a rectangular room that measures 4 m by 2.5 m. Now she must paint the ceiling of a room that measures 6 m by 10 m. She paints at a constant speed and without taking breaks.

If she starts painting the larger room at 9 am, what time will she finish?

A 1:30 pm

B 3 pm

C 4:30 pm

D 6 pm

15 The first floor of an office building is comprised of a number of rooms. The following is known about the rooms:

- The presentation room is the largest room.
- The kitchen and the meeting room are the same size.
- The bathroom only has one entrance.
- The computer room is connected to the kitchen.
- The boss's office has two entrances.

Of the following, which is the only possible floorplan?

A
Boss's office	Break room		Bathroom
Meeting		Presentation	
Computer			Kitchen

B
Presentation	Boss's office		Break room
	Kitchen	Computer	
Bathroom			Meeting

C
| Boss's office | Kitchen | Presentation | Bathroom |
| Meeting | Computer | | Break room |

D
Boss's office	Break room		Computer
Meeting		Presentation	
Bathroom			Kitchen

16 Locky and Remie both go to the same gym. Last week they did the same fitness test. The test had two parts. 50% of the score was for endurance and 50% was for strength. Locky and Remie just found out they got the same overall score in the fitness test.

Locky: 'If our scores for endurance were different from each other, then our scores for strength must have been different too.'

Remie: 'And if our scores for endurance were the same, then our scores for strength must have been the same too.'

If the information in the box is true, whose reasoning is correct?

A Locky only

B Remie only

C Both Locky and Remie

D Neither Locky nor Remie

17 The Ocean Sands local council has suggested closing down the dog park near the little penguin nesting sites.

Ms Wilson signed a petition to keep the dog park open and added this comment:

'If the dog park is closed, it will impact all dog owners in the area. So we must keep it open.'

Which assumption has Ms Wilson made in order to draw her conclusion?

A We should not do something that will impact dog owners in the area.

B The dog park near the little penguin nesting sites should not be closed.

C If the dog park is closed, it will impact all dog owners in the area.

D Ms Wilson likes to take her dog to the dog park near the little penguin nesting sites.

18 Three students were allowed to stay in the classroom at lunchtime to finish a project. One student drew on the whiteboard with permanent marker. When the teacher questioned the students, this is what they said:

Daniel: 'It wasn't me.'

Harry: 'I didn't do it.'

Pippa: 'Daniel did it.'

If only one of the three students is telling the truth and the other two are lying, which one of the following statements must then be true?

A Daniel is lying.

B Pippa is lying.

C Harry did not draw on the whiteboard.

D Pippa drew on the whiteboard.

19 Sam wants Charbel to go out to dinner with her. Charbel can't go out to dinner unless he finishes work before 5 pm but he might not finish before 5 pm because it's Christmas and he might have to work later than 5 pm.

Which of the following is **not** possible?

A Charbel finishes before 5 pm and they go out to dinner.

B Charbel has to work late and they don't go out to dinner.

C Charbel works late and they still go out to dinner.

D Charbel finishes early but they don't go out to dinner.

20 At a party, Brenda must choose to open one of five coloured boxes that are in a row on a table. There is one white, one black, one red, one yellow and one green. One of the boxes contains a necklace, one contains a camera and one contains a board game. The other two boxes are empty.

■ The black box is next to the green box, which is empty.

■ The red box and the green box are separated by two other boxes.

■ The white box is at one end of the row but the red box is not.

■ The camera is next to the yellow box.

■ The board game is next to the necklace and in one of the boxes at the end of the row.

Brenda opens the red box. What does she find?

A the necklace

B the camera

C the board game

D an empty box

IDENTIFYING THE MAIN IDEA
Page 1

1   **D is correct.** In this text the main idea comes from the first sentence and the fourth sentence, and option D best expresses it. The rest of the text gives reasons to believe this main idea.

   A and C are incorrect. This is supporting information for the main idea.

   B is incorrect. This information is not in the text so it cannot be the main idea.

2   **C is correct.** The main idea is that putting houseplants outside when it rains can be good for them. The rest of the text gives reasons to believe this idea.

   A and D are incorrect. This is supporting information for the main idea.

   B is incorrect. This information is not in the text so it cannot be the main idea.

IDENTIFYING A CONCLUSION THAT MUST BE TRUE
Page 3

1   **D is correct.** To answer this question you need to draw your own conclusion to determine which option is true. Because Yuki had proof of extensive theatrical experience and did exceptionally well in the drama improvisation challenge, she only had to pass the interview to be selected for the workshops.

   A is incorrect. People with no theatrical experience had to do exceptionally well in the interview and the drama improvisation challenge but Yuki did not do well in the drama improvisation challenge and only passed the interview.

   B is incorrect. Because Yuki did not do exceptionally well in the drama improvisation challenge, had no theatrical experience and only passed the interview, she would not have been selected for the workshops.

   C is incorrect. Because Yuki only passed the interview and did badly in the drama improvisation, she would not have been selected for the workshops.

2   **D is correct.** To answer this question, you need to draw your own conclusion to determine which option is true. The information in the question tells you that if a performer is good on the high wire, they are also good on the trapeze and (since they are good on the trapeze) they are also good at gymnastics but not juggling. Therefore it is reasonable to draw the conclusion that if Adele is not good on the highwire, she is also not good on the trapeze.

   A is incorrect. This cannot be true. You are told that anyone who is good on the highwire is also good on the trapeze but if you are good on the trapeze, you are not good at juggling. Hana cannot be good at juggling and on the highwire.

   B is incorrect. You are told that a performer who is good at juggling will not be good on the trapeze.

   C is incorrect. Just because the information says that a performer who is good on the high wire is also good on the trapeze, it does not automatically mean that a performer who is not good on the high wire will not be good on the trapeze.

IDENTIFYING A CONCLUSION THAT IS NOT POSSIBLE
Page 5

1   **B is correct.** This statement cannot be true. Ilja finished second but was slower than Bree so Bree must have been first to finish the test.

   A is incorrect. This statement could be true so we can't state it cannot be true.

   C is incorrect. This statement is true.

   D is incorrect. We don't know whether this statement is true or not, since we do not know how many questions Rose answered correctly. Therefore we can't state it cannot be true.

Name	Fastest time	No. of questions correct
Bree	1st	17
Ilja	2nd	18
Josh	3rd or 4th	19 or 20
Rose	3rd or 4th	Not known
Yifan	5th	20

2 D is correct. From the information given you can draw the conclusion that if Sofia's dad was in a bad mood, there was no way he would let Sofia go to the camping party. Therefore this conclusion cannot be true.

A is incorrect. This statement might be true. Even though Sofia didn't go shopping on Saturday, she might still have had another opportunity to buy the present and dad might not have been in a bad mood. If he was in a good mood, he might have let her go to the camping party.

B is incorrect. This statement might be true. The information tells us that if Sofia's dad was in a good mood, he might let her go to the camping party—not that he will definitely let her.

C is incorrect. This statement might be true. Sofia might have bought the present and her dad might still have been in a bad mood. Or he might have been in a good mood but still didn't let her go to the party.

IDENTIFYING EVIDENCE THAT LEADS TO A CONCLUSION

Page 7

1 To answer this question you need to judge which option helps you know the result. Remember that you are not being asked to work out the result.

C is correct. You are being asked to identify the evidence that will help you work out Marco's result in the spelling test. You are told that Nandi and Marco achieved the same mark in grammar and the same overall mark of 24 out of 30 but different marks in spelling and punctuation. The evidence in statement C is needed to work out that Marco's result in spelling is 7 out of 10.

A is incorrect. This statement does not provide any further evidence beyond that given in the question.

B and D are incorrect. This information does not help you work out Marco's result in spelling.

2 D is correct. Since everyone had to vote for two of the three gifts, knowing that no-one voted for both the concert tickets and the music store gift voucher tells you that everyone must have

voted for the book. D is the statement that allows you to work out the result of the vote: that the class will buy the book.

The other options are incorrect because they do not lead to a conclusion.

IDENTIFYING AN ASSUMPTION

Page 8

1 C is correct. For Zac's conclusion to hold, it must be assumed that Willow and Zac must not do anything to make Willow's brother angry: If Willow and Zac scratch the car, Willow's brother will be angry + Willow and Zac must not do anything to make Willow's brother angry means therefore Willow and Zac must not scratch the car.

A is incorrect. This is extra information and is immaterial to Zac's conclusion. It does not link the evidence to Zac's conclusion so it cannot be the assumption he has made: If Willow and Zac scratch the car, Willow's brother will be angry + Willow does not have a car of her own does not mean therefore Willow and Zac must not scratch the car.

B is incorrect. This is Zac's conclusion, not the missing assumption.

D is incorrect. This is the evidence or reasoning Zac has used to draw his conclusion.

2 A is correct. Mr Lees's conclusion is that the concrete median islands should not be installed. He has based this conclusion on the evidence or reasoning that if concrete median islands are installed, they will damage reversing cars. So for his conclusion to hold it must be assumed we should not do something that will cause damage to cars: If concrete median islands are installed, they will damage reversing cars + we should not do something that will cause damage to cars means therefore the concrete median islands should not be installed.

B is incorrect. This is Mr Lees's conclusion.

C is incorrect. This is the evidence or reasoning Mr Lees has used to draw his conclusion.

D is incorrect. This does not link Mr Lees's evidence or reasoning to his conclusion so it is not the assumption he has made based on that evidence.

IDENTIFYING **CORRECT REASONING**   Page 9

1   To answer this question you need to judge if the reasoning used to draw the conclusion is correct. If the reasoning is not correct or is flawed, then the conclusion drawn cannot be relied upon as true.

   C is correct. Both Alyce and Ned use correct reasoning. Alyce is correct to reason that if there are 25 votes, any food that gets 13 votes will win. Ned is correct to state that 25 votes and four choices means that any choice that receives 7 votes could be the winner.

   The other answers are incorrect by a process of elimination.

2   To answer this question you need to judge if the reasoning used to draw the conclusion is correct. If the reasoning is not correct or is flawed in some way, then the conclusion drawn cannot be relied upon as true.

   B is correct. Only Eddie has used correct reasoning to declare that crows have learned by watching other crows exhibit a behaviour that they then copy.

   A is incorrect. The rats in Lana's example learn for themselves as they individually work out how to release food.

   C is incorrect. Quolls learn to avoid eating cane toads because when they eat the small toads laced with toxin it makes them vomit. This is not behaviour learned from watching and copying other animals so Diana's reasoning is incorrect.

IDENTIFYING **FLAWED REASONING**   Page 11

1   **C is correct.** This option shows the mistake Xavier has made. He has added the one prize for People's Choice to the three prizes for first, second and third to conclude that there will be four prizes. Xavier has then assumed that the four prizes will go to four different pairs of owners and pets. He has not thought that the People's Choice winner might also come first, second or third—and therefore receive two of the prizes, meaning that only three pairs of owners and pets might get prizes.

   A is incorrect. The information tells us that each owner can enter only once and with only one pet. Therefore this sentence shows a mistake but it is not a mistake Xavier has made.

   B and D are incorrect. These statements might be true but they do not impact the number of prizes awarded and they are not mistakes Xavier has made.

2   **A is correct.** We know that any workers who were on cleaning duty on the last roster will definitely not be chosen for cleaning duty on the next roster. However, this doesn't mean that anyone who was not on cleaning duty on the last roster will definitely be chosen for cleaning duty on the next roster. So this sentence shows the flaw in Matilda's reasoning: that she might not be given cleaning duty next roster.

   B is incorrect. This sentence is a mistake since the supervisor said they definitely will not be chosen for cleaning duty on the next roster. However, it is not a mistake Matilda has made.

   C and D are incorrect. This sentence is not a mistake Matilda has made.

IDENTIFYING **ADDITIONAL EVIDENCE THAT STRENGTHENS AN ARGUMENT**   Page 13

1   **C is correct.** To answer this question you need to assess the statements to determine which one most strengthens the psychiatrist's argument. Start by identifying the argument: that children need to be allowed to relax and do nothing because overstimulation (sensory overload) is unhealthy.

   The statement that 'silence and time to do nothing gives the brain time to make thoughtful decisions rather than act impulsively' strengthens the argument.

   A is incorrect. This is a restatement of ideas already mentioned in the text.

   B and D are incorrect. These statements argue against the psychiatrist's argument.

2   **B is correct.** The argument is that we need to keep methane and carbon dioxide trapped in the permafrost and that bison can be used to help prevent the Arctic's permafrost from melting and releasing carbon dioxide and

methane gas into the atmosphere. The information that '37% of permafrost could be protected by bison' strengthens the argument to use bison in this way.

A is incorrect. This is a possible solution for the future but does not strengthen the argument about bison in the present day.

C and D are incorrect. These statements strengthen the argument that we need to protect permafrost, not that we need to use bison.

IDENTIFYING **ADDITIONAL EVIDENCE THAT WEAKENS AN ARGUMENT**   Page 15

1   **A is correct.** The principal argues that establishing a kitchen garden would be of little value to the school, yet a garden offers many opportunities to learn, including valuable life skills. So this statement contradicts, and therefore weakens, the principal's argument.

B and D are incorrect. The principal could use these statements as examples to strengthen her argument. It therefore does not weaken the argument.

C is incorrect. This statement neither strengthens nor weakens the argument, since we do not know the results of the survey.

2   **D is correct.** Finn's mum argues that every holiday should be a campervan holiday because campervanning is flexible and they don't need to plan anything. The statement that there are strict rules about where campervans can pitch and that most sites require you to book ahead most weakens this claim because it limits the scope of the argument that campervanning is flexible and does not require any planning.

A is incorrect. This statement could weaken a general argument in favour of the family always going on a driving/campervan holiday but it does not weaken the claim that campervanning is flexible.

B is incorrect. This statement strengthens the argument in favour of a campervanning holiday.

C is incorrect. This statement is irrelevant to the argument. It neither strengthens nor weakens the claim that campervanning is flexible.

IDENTIFYING **AN ARGUMENT THAT USES THE SAME STRUCTURE**   Page 17

1   **A is correct.** The argument that Jessica wants you to accept is that for Sebastian to become a paramedic he needs to study but he also needs particular personal attributes. If he doesn't have these personal attributes, he will never become a paramedic.

Another way to work out the structure of the argument is to say:

$X + Y = Z$ (Sebastian does X and Y and the result is Z).

The argument also shows that X without Y won't equal Z.

In option A, the argument Danielle wants you to accept is that she makes a great apple pie but for the pie crust to work out well she needs to refrigerate the pastry and if she doesn't refrigerate the pastry, the pie crust won't work out. Option A has the same structure as the argument in the box: $X + Y = Z$ and X without Y won't equal Z. (Great apple pie needs crust and refrigeration but without refrigeration the crust will not make a great pie.)

B is incorrect. This claim only has reasons to support the notion of companion planting. It does not suggest what will happen if you do not companion plant.

C is incorrect. This claim lists the skills and abilities that Praveena needs to become a successful magician. It does not include what will happen if she does not practise the particular skills; that is, without practice she won't become a good magician.

D is incorrect. This text only includes information to elaborate on a topic.

2   **D is correct.** The argument begins with an opening statement to define or introduce the topic of the Royal National Park, then makes a claim (it's a great park to visit) and lists evidence to support the claim (beautiful walking tracks and cycling trails). Option D begins with an opening statement to introduce the topic of the nursery frog and its habitat, then makes a claim that the nursery frog is at risk of extinction and gives evidence that increased temperatures make the frog's home uninhabitable.

A is incorrect. This option does not define the topic. It makes the claim that climate change is causing weather patterns to change, leading to heavier rain in some places and less rain in others.

B is incorrect. This option begins with an opening statement to introduce the topic of cane toads then makes the claim that cane toads are a problem. Then the text defines the way a biological control can cause problems in the environment and uses the cane toad as an example. This argument is more complex than the structure of the argument in the question.

C is incorrect. This option does not define the topic. It makes a claim where one thing causes another (drought impacts the ski season) and gives a reason (because there is less snow and also less water to produce fake snow).

ORDERING ITEMS IN ONE WAY　　Page 19

1　**C is correct.** Javier finished ahead of Zachary, who finished two places ahead of Yaz. Miriam also finished ahead of Zachary. This means Zachary came third and Yaz came fifth. Kara must have come fourth.

2　**C is correct.** Elena had the tastiest cake. Henry's cake was tastier than Felix's, whose cake was tastier than Grace's. Grace's cake was the least tasty.

ORDERING ITEMS IN TWO WAYS　　Page 20

1　**C is correct.** You need to work out who came first for creativity. Adrian scored higher than Ella and Mateo for creativity and Sophie scored lower than Ella. So Adrian had the top score for creativity.

Now you must work out where Adrian scored for technique. Adrian scored higher than Mateo but lower than Ella for technique. Sophie scored higher than Ella for technique. So Adrian was third for technique.

2　**C is correct.**

To solve this question we can create a simple table with two columns for the sprint and the long jump. We are told the person who came last in the sprint came second in the long jump. We don't know who this is but can write them in the table as a shape. Here we have used a

circle. We are then told the person who came first in the sprint came last in the long jump. We have used a square to represent this person.

Sprint	Long jump	
□		1st
	○	
○	□	4th

We are told that Shristi didn't come first or last in any event so she cannot be the circle or the square. She can't have won the long jump so she must have come third in the long jump.

Sprint	Long jump	
□	Liam	1st
Shristi	Javi	
Liam	Shristi	
Javi	□	4th

If Liam finished each event immediately ahead of Javi, Javi must be the circle as he is the only competitor that has a position immediately in front for Liam to occupy. Liam comes first in the long jump.

QUESTIONS USING 3D PUZZLES　　Page 21

1　**A is correct.** The solid that will fit looks like a 3D T with an extra bit attached to the top. This rules out B and D. The solid in C will have the extra bit on the wrong side. Looking at the given solid, you can picture the piece that fits together with it to make a cube.

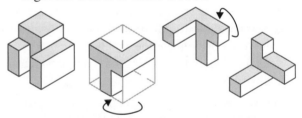

This piece can then be rotated to find the answer is A.

2　**D is correct.** You can see that the sloped section of the original solid does not go all the way to the top edge. This means the sloped section of the piece that fits will not go all the way to the bottom edge. This rules out A and B. If C is turned over, it is clear the sloped section will be on the wrong side of the solid to fit the two pieces together. Looking at the given solid, you can picture the piece that fits together with it to make a cube.

This piece can then be rotated to find the answer is D.

QUESTIONS ABOUT NETS AND DICE   Page 22

1   **B is correct.** If B were folded to create a cube, the white arrow would be pointing directly at the purple circle. This is not the case in the view of the cube shown.

2   **B is correct.**

ORDERING ITEMS BASED ON MANY FACTORS   Page 23

1   **A is correct.** Queenie made the black dress so we can rule out D immediately. If Paige didn't come in first or second, Madison came third and the green dress was fifth, then Paige came fourth. Nora must have come first and Queenie second, leaving Owen to come fifth.

Queenie made the black dress, Paige made the pink dress and Owen made the green one. If the orange one beat the white one, Nora made the orange dress and Madison made the white dress.

Place	Designer	Colour
1	Nora	orange
2	Queenie	black
3	Madison	white
4	Paige	pink
5	Owen	green

2   **A is correct.** Everyone plays Aussie rules except for one person. This person has red hair and must play cricket as well as soccer. Of the four people who play Aussie Rules, two must play soccer and two must play cricket as the same number of people play both sports.

So there are three people who play cricket and all of them have the same colour hair. We know one of them has red hair so all three must have red hair. This means at least three of the five friends have red hair and a maximum of two friends have brown hair. The answer is A.

QUESTIONS WITH STENCILS   Page 24

1   **A is correct.** The order in which the squares should be placed is shown below, as is the pile after each square is added.

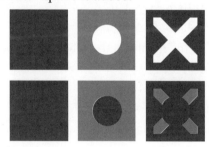

2   **B is correct.** The order in which the squares should be placed is shown below, as is the pile after each square is added.

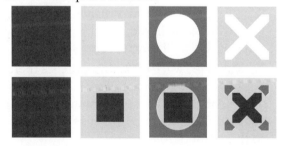

QUESTIONS THAT USE MULTIPLICATION   Page 26

1   **A is correct.** We can tell that one of the types of coins must be the 20c coins to make $7.20. There must be either one coin (20c) or six coins ($1.20) or 11 coins ($2.20), and so on.

But a 20c coin and a $1 coin won't add to $7.20. There must be six 20c coins and six $1 coins, as:
$6 \times \$0.20 + 6 \times \$1 = \$1.20 + \$6 = \$7.20$

Now add six 50c coins ($3) to $7.20 and Carlos has $10.20.

2 A is correct. Bella has the fewest number of 15-card packs. If she has one of those packs, she will have 4 packs of 4 (four times as many) and 7 packs of 10 (3 more than the number of 4-packs). 1 + 4 + 7 = 12, which is not 30 packs. So this cannot be the combination.

If she has 2 of those packs, she will only end up with 2 + 8 + 11 = 21 packs, which is not 30.

If she has 3 packs of 15, 12 packs of 4 and 15 packs of 10 she has 30 packs of cards.

$3 \times 15 + 12 \times 4 + 15 \times 10 = 45 + 48 + 150 = 243$

QUESTIONS THAT INVOLVE SWITCHING SYMBOLS
Page 27

1 D is correct. Tapping the highlighted symbols will produce A and also B.

Δ Ω Ψ Ψ Δ Ω Ω Δ Ψ Δ →
Δ Ω Ψ Ψ Δ Δ Δ Δ Ψ Δ

Tapping the highlighted symbols will produce B.

Δ Ω Ψ Ψ Δ Ω Ω Δ Ψ Δ →
Ψ Δ Ψ Ψ Δ Ω Ω Δ Ψ Δ

No move will produce D.

2 A is correct. What happens when two switches are flicked?

If two of the 'On' switches are switched to 'Off', then the number of 'Off' switches increases by 2. If two of the 'Off' switches are switched to 'On', then the number of 'Off' switches decreases by 2. If one of each is flicked, then the number showing 'Off' will stay the same.

For Pablo to switch off all the switches there must be an even number of switches showing 'Off' so he can decrease that number by 2s to get to 0. There are three switches showing 'Off' so this is not possible.

QUESTIONS THAT INVOLVE TWO SIDES OF A CARD
Page 28

1 B is correct. There are three cards with two sides. So there are six letters in all: A, E, N, R, T and W. If two letters are on the same card, they cannot both appear in the same word.

The letter A cannot be on the same card as the E, R, T or W, as it appears in the first two words alongside them. So the A and the N must be on the same card.

The letter E cannot be on the same card as the T or the W, as it appears in the second and third words alongside them. The E and the R must be on the same card.

The T and the W must be on the remaining card.

Option A (WET) is incorrect, as T and W cannot both be in the same word.

Option C (ANT) is incorrect, as A and N cannot both be in the same word.

Option D (EAR) is incorrect, as E and R cannot both be in the same word.

Option B (NEW) is correct.

2 A is correct. Of the numbers 1 to 8, there are two possible pairs that add up to 13. They are: 5 + 8 and 6 + 7. There are also two possible pairs that add up to 12. They are: 4 + 8 and 5 + 7.

You cannot use 5 and 8 for the card with a sum of 13 because either the 5 or the 8 would be needed for one of the cards with a sum of 12.

This means one card has the 6 and 7 on it, which sum to 13. One card has the 4 and 8 on it, which sum to 12.

The 5 and 2 are the only numbers left that can sum to 7. The 5 and 2 are on the same card.

QUESTIONS INVOLVING AREA
Page 29

1 D is correct. There will be exactly five tiles along the 1.25-m edge of the area, as 5 × 0.25 = 1.25 m. Six rows of tiles will cover 90 cm up the 1-m side of the area, as 6 × 0.15 = 0.90 m. This leaves 10 cm left out of the 15-cm side of the tile. So 5 cm, or one-third of it, will be chopped off, leaving the tile shown in option D.

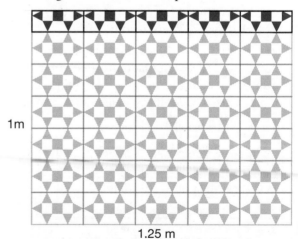

1m

1.25 m

2   **D is correct.** The lawn is twice as long and twice as wide. This creates a lawn area that is four times larger than the first lawn.

```
        40 m                    80 m
      ┌────────┐        ┌──────────────────┐
20 m  │        │        │                  │
      └────────┘   40 m │                  │
                        └──────────────────┘
```

So it will take Mitchell four times as long to mow the lawn. Instead of taking half an hour, it will take 2 hours. He will finish mowing the lawn 2 hours after 10 am at 12 noon.

SAMPLE TEST 1A
Page 31

> 1 D 2 A 3 B 4 C 5 B 6 D 7 B 8 C 9 A
> 10 B 11 B 12 C 13 D 14 C 15 A 16 D
> 17 B 18 C 19 B 20 D

1   Jacques only threw further than one other so he must have come third. Ivy was only beaten by one other so she must have come second. Magnus and Lily must then be first and fourth. If Magnus threw further than Lily, he must have come first.

2   The argument is that berries (and some other healthy foods) are too expensive for people to eat as often as recommended by nutritionists and so should be subsidised by governments. Option A strengthens this argument with additional supporting information.

B is incorrect. This statement weakens the argument because it argues against subsidising the berries due to the cost.

C is incorrect. This statement weakens the argument by claiming it could never get public approval anyway.

D is incorrect. This information is already provided in the text and so does not strengthen the argument.

3   From the information given, anyone who likes succulents likes cacti and (since they like cacti) they also like banksia but not roses. It is therefore not possible for someone who likes succulents to like roses so option B must be true.

The other options are incorrect. There is no evidence that they must be true.

4   Looking at the solid in C, you can picture the smaller piece that fits together with it.

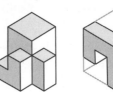 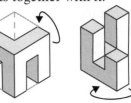

When rotated, this piece is the same as the solid in the question.

5   James reasons that a smaller car might travel fewer kilometres but he allows for the possibility that it could travel more kilometres than a bigger car.

A is incorrect. Xanthe cannot reasonably conclude that a smaller car must get more kilometres from a full charge. She has not considered other factors that might impact the number of possible kilometres on a car's charge, including the size of the battery.

C and D are incorrect by a process of elimination.

6   The order in which the squares should be placed is shown below, together with the pile after each square is added.

7   If Kiara has one $50 note, she has three $20 notes and five $10 notes. 1 + 3 + 5 = 9 which is not 16 notes. This cannot be the case.

If Kiara has two $50 notes, she has six $20 notes and eight $10 notes. This adds up to 16 notes. So you can now calculate how much money this is.

2 × $50 + 6 × $20 + 8 × $10 = 300

Kiara has $325 so the $5 notes make up the $25 left. There are five $5 notes.

8   The information tells you any horse that likes dates likes carrots and if it likes carrots, it also likes apples.

A is incorrect. It cannot be true that if Roxie likes raisins, she also likes apples because you are told that a horse which likes carrots likes apples but not raisins.

B is incorrect. This cannot be true because no horse that eats carrots also eats raisins.

D is incorrect. This cannot be true because if a horse likes apples, it also likes carrots.

9 Helen has mistakenly decided that using electronic devices prevents people from falling asleep but has not recognised that students having difficulty falling asleep might be trying to use electronic devices to help them sleep.

B is incorrect. Television viewing is irrelevant to the question.

C is incorrect. Helen has not considered whether students are allowed to use the devices at bedtime.

D is incorrect. Whether some students are more interested than others in electronic devices is irrelevant to the mistake Helen has made.

10 If there are only three switches showing 'On', it will take one move as Gustav can just flick these three switches. There are four switches showing 'On' so he cannot do it in one move.

The aim is to reduce the number of switches saying 'On' to three so that switching them all off is the last move. To do this Gustav can flick two of the switches showing 'On' to 'Off' and one of the 'Off' switches to 'On'. This is one move, leaving only one more move to switch the three 'On' switches to 'Off'. It will take a total of two moves.

11 Sonja's argument is that almonds are not a sustainable crop in Australia because they require too much water so hazelnuts should be grown instead of almonds. The fact that almond trees grow well in some wetter parts of Australia weakens her argument.

A and C are incorrect. The claims that almonds are healthier and taste better are irrelevant to Sonja's argument.

D is incorrect. The fact that hazelnuts need less water and grow in poorer soils than almonds strengthens Sonja's argument.

12 Option C cannot be true. Hilda and Ben must like pop least because they like rap more than pop and no-one likes rock least.

A is incorrect. It could be true that three people—Hilda, Ben and Ash—like rap best. Hilda and Ben must like rap best. Ash likes rap better than rock so could like rap best. Gitte must like rap least because she likes pop more than rock and no-one likes rock least.

B is incorrect. Hilda and Ben like rap best.

D is incorrect. Hilda and Ben like pop least.

13 **A is incorrect.** Kirsty is incorrect in stating that Bianca must not have attended two training sessions during the week. Bianca might have been dropped because she had not been playing as well as others on the team.

B is incorrect. Amy cannot assert that Bianca will definitely not be dropped from the team if she attends practice and improves her performance. Other players may have improved more than Bianca or might have been playing better than her.

C is incorrect by a process of elimination.

14 There are three cards with two sides. So there are six letters in all: A, E, G, I, L and P. If two letters are on the same card, they cannot both appear in the same word.

The letter P cannot be on the same card as the A, E, G or I as it appears in PIG and APE alongside them. So the P and the L must be on the same card. For similar reasons G and A are on the same card and E and I are on the same card.

Option A (LEG) can be made as it is just the letters of GEL backwards.

Option B (PEG) can be made as the card with the L on it can be turned over to show the P and we know LEG can be made.

Option D (ALE) can be made as the card with the P on it can be turned over to show the L and we know APE can be made.

Option C (GAP) is the correct answer as G and A cannot appear in the same word as they are on two sides of the same card.

15 The purple circle should be attached to the left-hand side of the purple arrow if the arrow is pointing up. This is not the case in A.

16 The main idea the writer wants you to know or accept is that Monarch butterflies are under threat of extinction due to loss of milkweed along their migration routes.

The other options are incorrect. These are all facts in the text but not the main idea.

17 You need to work out who completed the games in the shortest amount of time.

Lukas was slower than Xavier, who was slower than Maya. Emma was faster than Maya. So Emma was the fastest (or the person who finished games in the shortest time).

Emma finished the competition ahead of Lukas, who was ahead of Xavier. Emma finished behind Maya.

Emma finished in second position.

18 Tim has decided that because Grandma Dorothy is grumpy and short tempered, he will request a different carer for her. In order to reach this conclusion he has assumed that Camilla is the cause of Grandma's behaviour.

A is incorrect. It might be a good idea to speak to Grandma and ask if anything is bothering her but this is not the assumption that led Tim to his decision/conclusion.

B is incorrect. It might be true that Grandma would like a new carer but Tim does not even know if the carer is the cause of Grandma's change in attitude and this is not the assumption that has led to Tim's decision.

D is incorrect. Tim has not assumed this. He has, instead, assumed that the carer is to blame.

19 A room that is 2.5 m by 3.5 m would be covered perfectly by full-sized tiles. The difference between 2.9 m and 2.5 m is 0.4 m. The difference between 3.85 m and 3.5 m is 0.35 m. The tile will have the dimensions of these differences.

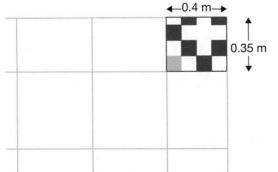

20 First you need to work out the order in which the bands performed as the prizes are linked to this in the information you are given.

Bravo Billy (B) performed second and Cheeky Charlies (C) must have performed third or fourth as they didn't perform first or last.

Alpha Tauri (A) performed straight after Delta Force (D). They did not perform third and fourth as Cheeky Charlies (C) must have performed in one of those slots. So they performed fourth and fifth, meaning Echo Point (E) performed first.

So the order must be:

Band	E	B	C	D	A

The band that performed fourth won first prize.

The band that performed first came second and the band that performed second came third.

Band	E	B	C	D	A
Prize	second	third		first	

Cheeky Charlies did not win a prize.

SAMPLE TEST 1B Page 36

> **1** B **2** C **3** B **4** B **5** C **6** A **7** D **8** C **9** A
> **10** D **11** D **12** A **13** C **14** A **15** C **16** D
> **17** B **18** B **19** B **20** A

1 If Nyjah finishes ahead of Preston but two places behind Ollie, you can place those three easily:

O   ?   N   P

One of the other skaters must be placed where the question mark is and the other can be placed ahead of Ollie, between Nyjah and Preston or after Preston.

When you are told that Mick finishes ahead of Ollie, you can write in M:

M   O   ?   N   P

It is clear that Quinton finished in third place.

2 Looking at the solid in C, you can picture the piece that fits together with it to make a cube.

This piece can be rotated to make the solid from the question.

3 From the information given we know that
1 damma = 5 cammas = 25 bammas. As we also
know 2 ammas = 1 bamma then we can work
out that 25 bammas = 50 ammas.

So the full equation is:
1 damma = 5 cammas = 25 bammas = 50 ammas.

We want to know how many ammas are in a
camma: 5 cammas = 50 ammas.

Divide the numbers in the equation by 5, giving
1 camma = 10 ammas.

4 For Peter to attend the party he must have
finished his homework. The fact that Jordan did
not attend the party does not mean he didn't
finish his homework. He might have finished his
homework but decided not to go to the party.
The information does not tell you that both
boys wanted to attend the party.

The other options are incorrect by a process of
elimination.

5 The information states that attending the
audition is the first step in joining the choir.
There are likely further requirements. Jackson
can't declare that Sophia will definitely be
accepted into the choir simply because she
attended the audition.

A and B are incorrect. Even though they are
unlikely to be true they are not the mistake
Jackson has made.

D is incorrect. Based on information you are
given, this is not true. Also it is not the mistake
Jackson has made.

6 The order in which the squares should be
placed is shown below, together with the pile
after each square is added.

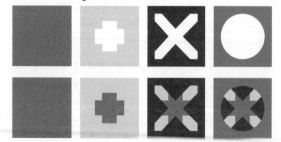

7 It is true that the red lights cannot be on when
the white lights are off.

The other options are incorrect. These options
are not possible.

8 The argument is that the company operates
sustainably and repurposes waste materials to
help prevent further climate change. The fact
that the company sells bags online globally
means these goods are posted around the world.
This is the opposite of shopping locally and
weakens the argument that the company
operates 100% sustainably in preventing
further climate change.

A is incorrect. This statement is true and
strengthens the argument.

B is incorrect. This statement might be true but
it neither strengthens nor weakens the
argument about preventing climate change.

D is incorrect. This statement might be true but
it neither strengthens nor weakens the
argument about preventing climate change.

9 It is possible to find B inside the string if the
two shapes selected are tapped.

It is possible to find C inside the string if the
two shapes selected are tapped.

It is possible to find D inside the string if the
two shapes selected are tapped.

The only way to get three triangles in a row is
by changing the shapes selected. This leaves a
circle as the fourth shape. A is not possible.

10 Yana is correct in stating that the driver might
have been on the phone. Emily is correct in
stating that there are many reasons for being
pulled over by the police but the most likely
reason while driving on a motorway is speeding.
Neither Yana nor Emily are strongly assertive.
Each person allows for alternative reasons for
the police to pull over a driver.

A and B are incorrect. Layne is incorrect in stating the driver can't have been wearing a seatbelt. Layne could have reasoned that the driver might not have been wearing a seat belt but Layne's statement that the driver can't have been wearing a seat belt is too strongly assertive and leaves no room for doubt or other options.

C is incorrect. Zane is incorrect in stating the driver must have been speeding. Zane could only accurately reason that the driver might have been speeding.

11 Of the numbers 1 to 8 there are three possible pairs that add up to 10. They are 2 + 8, 3 + 7 and 4 + 6. There are also three possible pairs that add up to 11. They are 3 + 8, 4 + 7 and 5 + 6.

You cannot use 3 and 8 for the card with a sum of 11 because either the 3 or the 8 would be needed for one of the cards with a sum of 10.

Similarly you cannot use 4 and 7 for the card with a sum of 11. One of those numbers must be used for a card with a sum of 10.

This means one card has the 6 and 5 on it, which sum to 11. One card has the 2 and 8 on it, one card has the 3 and 7 on it, and the last card has the 4 and 1 on it.

It is only possible to see one side of a card at a time so:

A is incorrect as it includes the 5 and the 6.
B is incorrect as it includes the 1 and the 4.
C is incorrect as it includes the 7 and the 3.

12 The structure of the given text is an introductory (thesis) statement, followed by three reasons to support the thesis and finally a call to action. Text A begins with a thesis statement about the importance of the spectacled flying fox. It then gives three reasons to protect the flying fox and concludes with a call to action.

The other options are incorrect. These texts have different structures.

13 The white arrow needs to be connected to the purple circle and pointing away from it. This is not the case in A or D so we can rule them out. The purple square needs to be connected to the arrow but must be on the right side of it if we look at the arrow pointing upwards. This is

not the case in B, where it is on the left. So we can rule out B.

14 You are not told explicitly where each person stands compared to one another but by using small shapes to represent each person in a simple table you can work out the answer.

The person who won the judges' prize is represented by the square.

The person who won the public prize is represented by the circle.

The person who came third in the judges' prize is represented by the triangle.

The final person will go in the blank space.

Judges'	Public	
□	○	1st
	△	
△	□	
○		4th

We are told Siddharth came second in the public prize so he is the triangle.

You are then told that Niamh is beaten by Fong in both prizes. There is only one possible way this can happen: if Fong is the square and Niamh is in the blank space.

The triangle cannot be either Niamh or Fong as it beats only the circle in the judges' prize but loses to it in the public prize. The circle similarly cannot be either of them as it is beaten by everyone in the judges' prize but by no-one in the public prize.

So once Fong and Niamh are put in, we can replace the circle with Elijah. The person who came last in the judges' prize is clearly Elijah.

Judges'	Public	
Fong	Elijah	1st
Niamh	Siddharth	
Siddharth	Fong	
Elijah	Niamh	4th

15 When the second train leaves at 10 am, the first train has already travelled 5 h of a 12-h journey. So it has 7 h left until it arrives in Sydney. This

means that at 10 am the trains are 7 h away from each other. If they travel towards each other at the same speed, they will pass each other exactly halfway along that 7-h journey. So they will pass each other 3.5 hours after 10 am which is 1:30 pm.

16 The argument is that virtual travel has benefits for people of all levels of physical ability but especially for people with disabilities for whom travelling to challenging destinations is impossible.

A is incorrect. This statement strengthens the argument in favour of virtual travel but does not apply specifically to people with disabilities.

B is incorrect. This statement weakens the argument that virtual travel is as good as actual travel for people with disabilities.

C is incorrect. This aspect of virtual travel is a drawback so it weakens the argument.

17 Option B cannot be true. Damon will compete in the individual events unless he is successful at the trials in Brisbane and secures a place in the team competition.

A is incorrect. It is true that three athletes will be selected by the National Athletics Committee.

C is incorrect. It is true that two athletes will be named as individual competitors.

D is incorrect. It is true that Damon could compete as an individual competitor based on his own body of work.

18 The argument is that people should not drive in blizzard conditions because of poor visibility and an increased risk of road accidents. Option B strengthens the argument by giving an extra reason for avoiding driving in a blizzard: If you are in a road accident, it's more difficult for rescue services to reach your vehicle.

A is incorrect. This is a restatement of the main idea in the text so it does not strengthen the argument.

C is incorrect. Although it is true, this statement is about pedestrians in a blizzard and not about driving in a blizzard.

D is incorrect. Although it is true, this is not the statement that most strengthens the argument

not to drive in a blizzard because of the risk of being involved in an accident.

19 Option B cannot be true because competitors playing for the all-round athlete points trophy cannot win individual sport trophies.

A is incorrect. It is true that no competitor competing for the all-round athlete trophy can win a trophy for the basketball event or any other individual event.

C is incorrect. It is true that if a competitor is not competing for the all-round athlete trophy, they cannot win points for placing first, second or third in an event.

D is incorrect. It is possible that a club with an outstanding girls' team could win the all-round athlete trophy.

20 When Vince writes +$@&# for his age he is writing each letter of the word eight. From this you can see that # is t and + is e.

There are only four numbers that have three letters in them when spelt out: one, two, six and ten. The code starts with a t but the second letter is not an e so Vince must be two years younger than his brother.

His brother must be 10 years old.

SAMPLE **TEST 2A**   Page 42

1 A 2 A 3 D 4 D 5 A 6 C 7 A 8 A 9 C
10 C 11 B 12 C 13 D 14 D 15 B 16 C
17 B 18 A 19 A 20 D

1 Jasmine makes fewer baskets than Leo but more than Hannah, who makes more than Isaac.

The order of those four is: Leo, Jasmine, Hannah, Isaac.

If Geoff came third, the final order is: Leo, Jasmine, Geoff, Hannah, Isaac.

Hannah comes fourth.

2 Shona's mistake is that, no matter how many games were played, either one of the players may have played unusually well this week so just because Georgia won ten games and even though they each win roughly the same number of games against each other, it does not mean that 20 games must have been played this week.

B and C are incorrect. These statements are true but are not the mistake Shona has made.

D is incorrect. This is unlikely to be true and is not the mistake Shona has made.

3 Option D is not possible because Toni is busy on Saturday and is unavailable to help.

The other options are incorrect. Each of these options is possible.

4 Looking at the original solid, you can picture the piece that fits together with it to make a cube.

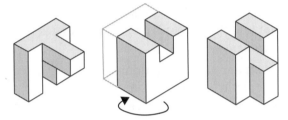

This piece can be rotated to find the answer is C.

5 The cleaner turns on the television on days the carer does not. The carer does not turn on the television on Saturdays and Sundays. The cleaner does not work on Saturdays but does work on Sundays so today must be Sunday.

B and C are incorrect by a process of elimination.

D is incorrect. There is no information to support the conclusion that the carer is unexpectedly away.

6 The order in which the squares should be placed is shown below, together with the pile after each square is added.

7 There are 6 fingots in 1 hengol, as $2 \times 3 = 6$. If you have 5 hengols, you will have 30 fingots, as $5 \times 6 = 30$. This means that 5 hengols have the same value as 1 ingol.

8 If it is true that whoever stole the tree must have had a motive for taking it, then it must also be true that if Lily did not steal the tree, she cannot have had a motive.

B is incorrect. Just because Lily had an opportunity to steal the tree and knew it was there, it does not mean she must have taken it.

C is incorrect. This statement is not logical.

D is incorrect. It is illogical to say that if Lily did not have a motive, she must have taken the tree.

9 Lana's argument is that the majority of students have no need for maths beyond Year 6. Her argument is contradicted by option C which states that education institutions often require some level of maths for entry so it would be a disadvantage to not study maths in high school.

A and B are incorrect. These statements support Lana's argument.

D is incorrect. This statement neither supports nor contradicts Lana's argument.

10 It is possible to find A inside the string if the two shapes selected are tapped.

It is possible to find B inside the string if the two shapes selected are tapped.

It is possible to find D inside the string if the two shapes selected are tapped.

C is not possible after only one move.

11 The argument is that peanut paste is a cost-effective treatment for malnutrition in children in areas of drought, war or natural disaster. The information that peanut paste is cost effective to produce, store, transport and distribute strengthens this argument.

A and C are incorrect. These statements provide additional information but do not strengthen the argument that peanut paste is a cost-effective treatment for malnutrition.

D is incorrect. This statement is a call to action that is not presented in the text so does not strengthen the argument.

12 It is not possible that Evie said she'd drive to Sydney with Sharna at Easter if Sharna was a poor driver. Evie announced that it would be the last time she ever takes Sharna to Sydney by car if Sharna is a poor driver on the trip at Christmas.

The other options are incorrect. These options are possible.

13 There are four cards with two sides. So there are eight letters in all: A, I, H, N, O, P, S and W. If two letters are on the same card, they cannot both appear in the same word.

The letter S cannot be on the same card as the A, H, N, O, P or W, as it appears in the words WASH, SWAP and SWAN alongside them. So the S and the I must be on the same card. This means they cannot appear in a word together.

For similar reasons W and P must be on two sides of the same card so they cannot appear in a word together.

The other two cards are A and O, and H and N.

Option C (SHIP) is incorrect. It contains both an S and an I.

Option B (WASP) and option A (PAWN) are incorrect as they both contain a W and a P.

Option D (SNOW) is the correct answer.

14 The proverb means it's best to deal with problems when they are small rather than allow them to grow bigger when they will require more effort to resolve; that is, one stitch in a timely manner saves needing nine stitches later on.

A is incorrect. While the proverb advises people not to put off tasks that need doing, it is not about worrying for nine times longer.

B is incorrect. The proverb might apply to sewing up a small rip in clothing before the rip grows larger but the proverb has a wider application.

C is incorrect. You can tell by the way Aunty uses the proverb that it does not apply to doing things well, only to doing them as soon as they need doing or in a timely manner.

15 The purple arrow should be pointing towards the purple circle. This is not the case in B. Option B is the correct answer.

16 It was possible to get into the course with Alyssa's excellent personal attributes if she had passed the thinking skills test.

If Alyssa had failed the thinking skills test, she would not have been accepted into the course even though her personal attributes were excellent.

A is incorrect. Alyssa only needed to pass the thinking skills test.

B is incorrect. Alyssa did not need to pass the maths test if she passed the thinking skills test.

D is incorrect. This cannot be the reason as you are told that Alyssa's personal attributes were excellent.

17 From the second and third statements you can see that Ish has fewer stamps than Niall, who has fewer than Regan. This means Ish has the third most or the fewest stamps. The answer must be either Ish or Ethan. You must find out where Ethan fits to work out which.

Niall has more coins than Regan but fewer coins than Ish. So Ish has more coins than these two. From the third statement you can see Ethan has more coins than Ish. So Ethan must have the most coins. This also means he must have the most stamps. This means Ish has the fewest stamps.

18 Nandita correctly reasons that because Eddie's hair was dyed pink he must have got a good end-of-year report.

B is incorrect. Hailey might have achieved a good end-of-year report but decided not to dye her hair pink.

C and D are incorrect by a process of elimination.

19 A room that is 2 m by 2.5 m would be covered perfectly by full-sized tiles. The difference between 2.2 m and 2 m is 0.2 m. The difference between 2.7 m and 2.5 m is 0.2 m. The tile will have the dimensions of these differences. You can see this below.

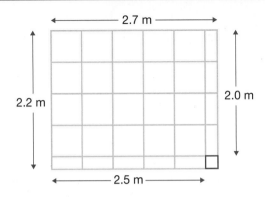

2.7 m

2.2 m   2.0 m

2.5 m

20 Neither P nor Q is grey or flecked. If two puppies must be grey, two of the puppies R, S and T must be grey. Similarly two of them must be flecked. This means at least one of them is both grey and flecked. The answer is D.

The other options are all possible, but it is not the case that they must be true.

SAMPLE TEST 2B

Page 47

1 A **2** C **3** C **4** C **5** D **6** B **7** D **8** C **9** B
10 C **11** A **12** D **13** D **14** B **15** A **16** D
17 A **18** D **19** C **20** D

1 If Finlay finished in third position, this means Cameron and Garth must finish in second and fourth position, as Cameron is two places ahead of Garth and neither can be in third position.

Emma must then come in fifth as she finished below Finlay. Desh must come first, the only position left to be taken.

2 Looking at the original solid, you can picture the piece that fits together with it to make a cube.

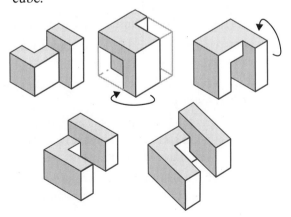

This piece can be rotated to find the answer is C.

3 Mica's argument is that 16 and 17-year-olds should be allowed to vote. Statement C weakens the argument that they should be given the vote.

A is incorrect. This statement does not address the issue of lowering the voting age.

B is incorrect. This statement could be true but it could apply to any age group and does not specifically address the argument.

D is incorrect. This statement strengthens the argument to lower the voting age.

4 Arabella has mistakenly assumed that the cyclist who wins 'Top of the Mountain' will not be a cyclist who places first, second or third in the race. Four medals may be awarded to three winners. Any of the first, second or third placed cyclists could also win 'Top of the Mountain'.

A is incorrect. There is no information regarding a 'Best and Fairest' medal.

B is incorrect. You are told there is a 'Top of the Mountain' medal to be won so there must be a mountain in the race.

D is incorrect. This is likely to be true but it is not the mistake Arabella has made.

5 The order in which the squares should be placed is shown below, together with the pile after each square is added.

6 Only Nikita shows correct reasoning. The information tells you that to be a great chef you must listen well to, and accept, instructions. Nikita says that Tariq cannot do this so she reasons that he'll struggle working in a kitchen.

Otto is incorrect because he cannot reasonably state that just because Bianca has a passion for food, can follow instructions and is well-organised she's certain to make a great chef.

The other options are incorrect by a process of elimination.

7 If the pizza was delivered at 8 pm by someone other than Celia's favourite delivery driver, then it must have been a day when her favourite driver was not working. This could only be on Mondays and Tuesdays any time or on Wednesday after 5 pm. D is the only option that fits these criteria.

The other options are incorrect. Celia's favourite delivery driver works until 9 pm on Thursdays, Fridays, Saturdays and Sundays so would have delivered the pizza.

8 You need to find out how many there are of each colour chip. Knowing there are only 20 chips in total means you can use trial and error to find out. The blue tokens are fewest as there are three times as many purple, and five more red than blue.

If you have 1 blue, you will have 3 purple and 6 red: $1 + 3 + 6 = 10$, not 20. So this cannot be the case.

If you have 2 blue, you will have 6 purple and 7 red: $2 + 6 + 7 = 15$, not 20. So this cannot be the case.

If you have 3 blue, you will have 9 purple and 8 red: $3 + 9 + 8 = 20$

$$Total points = 3 \times 10 + 9 \times 5 + 8 \times 3$$
$$= 30 + 45 + 24$$
$$= 99 \text{ points}$$

9 The third card cannot have a cross on one side and a circle on the other side. This rules out A.

The second card was flipped over twice so will still show a circle. This rules out D.

The first card is flipped over three times, which is the same as flipping it over just once. As it starts off showing the blank side, it cannot also show a blank side after being flipped over. This rules out C.

10 If Jeremy was faster than Josef in the heat and Josef was one of three swimmers in the heat to make it into the semifinals, then Josef would have had to come second or third and Jeremy first or second.

A is incorrect. Josef could not have come first if Jeremy was faster than him.

B is incorrect. This could be true but the question asks which statement must be true if Josef qualifies for the semifinals.

D is incorrect. You are told that Jeremy swam faster than Josef so they could not have tied for first place.

11 All numbers on the cards add up to the same thing: $1 + 2 + 3 + 4 + 5 + 6 + 7 + 8 = 36$. So the sums of the cards must add up to 36. If three of the cards add to $9 + 10 + 11 = 30$, the other card must sum to 6, as $36 - 30 = 6$.

The only two combinations that make 6 are $1 + 5$ and $2 + 4$ but we are told that 2 and 4 are not on the same card. So it must be true that 1 and 5 are on the same card.

12 If the severity of any penalty (fining people or sending them to jail) does not deter people from committing crimes, then it is incorrect to reason that not fining people or threatening them with jail has an impact on crime rates.

A is incorrect. This statement is true and is stated in the text so it does not show incorrect reasoning.

B is incorrect. This statement is true and uses correct reasoning.

C is incorrect. This statement is logical and could be true. Therefore it does not show incorrect reasoning.

13 The purple arrow must be connected to and pointing to the purple square. This is not the case in B or C. The white arrow must point at the grey arrow. This is not the case in A.

14 Ms Chen did not collect the times of all students running the course prior to undertaking her experiment so she couldn't determine the average speed of each group. The students who were given the red jelly may have been faster on average at cross country anyway.

A is incorrect. This could be true but it was not the mistake Ms Chen has made.

C is incorrect. The information is irrelevant to Ms Chen's study.

D is incorrect. Ms Chen used averages to draw her conclusion so it's irrelevant how many students were in each group.

15 To solve this question we can create a simple table with two columns for comics and action figures.

We are told the person who has the most comics has the second-most action figures. We don't know who this is but can write them in the table as a shape. Here we have used a circle.

We are then told the person who has the fewest comics has the most action figures. We have used a square to represent this person.

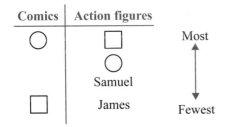

Comics	Action figures	
◯	▢	Most
	◯	
▢		Fewest

We are told James has more comic books than Amelia but fewer than Lily. This means he cannot have either the most or the fewest comics. So he cannot be the circle or the square.

If Samuel cannot have the most or fewest of anything, he also cannot be the circle or the square. He also cannot have the fewest action figures. So he must have the third-most action figures and James must have the fewest.

Comics	Action figures	
◯	▢	Most
	◯	
	Samuel	
▢	James	Fewest

16 If it takes Lillian 60 minutes and Howard 20 minutes to cover the same distance, Howard is travelling three times as fast as Lillian, as 20 × 3 = 60. So Howard covers three times the distance that Lillian covers in the same length of time.

Howard will travel three-quarters of the distance between the towns in the same time that Lillian travels one-quarter of the distance.

So we can divide the trip between the towns into four parts. Each part will take Howard 5 minutes and Lillian 15 minutes. They will pass each other after 15 minutes at 10:15 am.

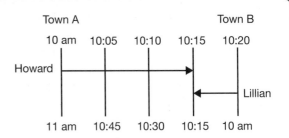

17 Statement A most strengthens the argument because it points to the broad categories of therapy provided by music or sounds.

The other options are incorrect. These statements are all true and each strengthens the argument in support of the benefits of sound or music therapy. However, they each only refer to one area of benefit.

18 Rowan wants a medium-soft mattress. If Horizon Air is the softest mattress and Horizon Cloud the least soft, then the two medium-soft mattresses for Rowan to choose from are Cosy-up Comfort and Dreamsleeper. Rowan is on a budget so he needs the cheaper of these two. You are told that Dreamsleeper is more expensive than Cosy-up Comfort so Rowan uses correct reasoning when he chooses to buy a Cosy-up Comfort mattress.

A is incorrect. Ashley needs the lowest-priced soft mattress. Horizon Air is the most expensive mattress so she uses incorrect reasoning.

B is incorrect. Conrad doesn't want the softest mattress so he uses flawed reasoning when he chooses Horizon Air as it is the softest mattress.

C is incorrect. Nikky uses incorrect reasoning when she chooses the Dreamsleeper because it is not the softest mattress available nor is it the most expensive mattress available. The softest and most expensive would be the Horizon Air.

19 The information tells us that everyone in favour of a disco also liked a bowling party and no-one who liked a bowling party liked laser tag. So it is reasonable to draw the conclusion that if Ava is in favour of a disco, she also likes a bowling party and so does not like laser tag.

A is incorrect. The information tells us that everyone who liked a disco liked a bowling party.

B is incorrect. There is not enough information to draw this conclusion so we cannot say it must be true.

D is incorrect. The information tells us that everyone who liked a bowling party also liked a beach party but it doesn't follow that everyone who likes a beach party also likes a bowling party.

20 B is incorrect as jazz has a double letter. There is no repeated symbol in Prue's answer. The code for Prue shows you that r is ^ and u is #. Neither of these symbols are shown so there can be no r or u in the answer. This rules out soul and rock as possible answers. The answer is D.

SAMPLE TEST 3A

Page 52

1 C 2 B 3 D 4 B 5 B 6 B 7 A 8 C 9 D
10 D 11 A 12 A 13 B 14 B 15 C 16 C
17 D 18 C 19 A 20 D

1 If Gabriel finished two places behind Mia, Mia must have come in first, second or third place. But Isabella finished ahead of Mia so Mia must have come in second or third. But Oscar finished in second place so Mia came third.

Isabella finished in first place, Oscar came second, Mia came third and Gabriel came fifth. This means the only position for Sandy is fourth.

2 Only Jarrah's reasoning is correct. Since the debating team competes every Wednesday and Mr Brown always gives homework on Thursday if the debating team loses, then if today is Thursday and he didn't give homework it must be true that the team won.

A is incorrect. Chloe's reasoning has a flaw. Just because Mr Brown gives homework when the debating team loses, it does not follow that he doesn't give homework at any other time. Therefore it is possible that Mr Brown gave homework even though the debating team won so Chloe cannot say the team must have lost.

C and D are incorrect by a process of elimination.

3 From the information given, you can draw the conclusion that if the whole band does not learn the new piece, then the festival trip will not be a success. And if it is not a success, then Ms Webster will not let them have the trip to the theme park at the end of term. So this conclusion is not possible.

A is incorrect. This statement might be true. Just because the text says the festival trip will be cancelled if they don't all come to band practice, it does not mean there cannot be some other reason why the festival trip might have been cancelled.

B is incorrect. This statement might be true if not all the students came to band practice that afternoon.

C is incorrect. This statement might be true. The information tells us that the festival trip will not be a success if the band does not learn the new piece. However, meeting that condition does not guarantee the festival trip will be a success.

4 Looking at the original solid, you can picture the piece that fits together with it to make a cube.

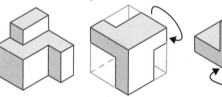

This piece can be rotated to find the answer is B.

5 Option B best expresses the main idea. The rest of the text supports this main idea by giving more information about how brinicles form and what happens when they spread.

A is incorrect. This background information is used in the introduction but it is not the main idea. The main idea is about brinicles.

C is incorrect. This information is not in the text (the text says the **reader** may not have heard of brinicles) so it cannot be the main idea.

D is incorrect. This statement supports the main idea.

6 Leo gives an opinion and then three reasons to support it. In option B Lina gives an opinion and three reasons to support that opinion.

A is incorrect. Elaine only gives one reason to support her claim that she doesn't like funny books.

C is incorrect. Ari begins by providing evidence and then concludes with an opinion.

D is incorrect. Ethan states an opinion, provides some evidence, then restates his opinion.

7 The order in which the squares should be placed is shown below, together with the pile after each square is added.

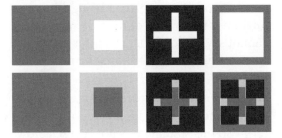

8 There are three times as many $5 notes as $50 notes so the answer must be a multiple of 3 (either 3, 6, 9, 12, 15, etc.). While this does not help us rule out any answers in this question, it is a good observation to make for other questions.

You also know the answer must be an odd number to get $345, as an even number will give a number ending in 0. So we can rule out B.

If there are fifteen $5 notes, there are five $50 notes and the total amount of money from just these notes is $15 \times \$5 + 5 \times \$50 = \$325$, which doesn't leave room for the $10 and $20 notes. So the answer must be 3 or 9.

Here is where things get tricky. If there are three $5 notes, there is one $50 note and they total $65. This means the other $280 must be comprised of the $10 and $20 notes, which seems possible, until you remember that there must be twice as many $20 notes as $10 notes. These notes can only make $50 (one $10 and two $20) or $100 (two $10 and four $20) or $150, $200, $250, $300, etc.; that is, they can only make multiples of $50.

The answer is therefore 9, which is C.

There are 9 $5 notes, 3 $10 notes, 6 $20 notes and 3 $50 notes.

$$\begin{aligned} \text{Total} &= 9 \times \$5 + 3 \times \$10 + 6 \times \$20 + 3 \times \$50 \\ &= \$45 + \$30 + \$120 + \$150 \\ &= \$345 \end{aligned}$$

9 This statement most strengthens the argument since the survey found there was a need for the new park.

A is incorrect. This statement neither strengthens nor weakens the council's argument that the bike park is a better use for the site.

B is incorrect. This statement weakens the argument rather than strengthens it.

C is incorrect. This statement would strengthen an argument for the previous plan to construct a garden.

10 It is possible to find A inside the string if the two shapes selected are tapped.

It is possible to find B inside the string if the two shapes selected are tapped.

It is possible to find C inside the string if the two shapes selected are tapped.

The only way to get three squares in a row is by changing the shapes selected. This leaves a circle as the fifth shape. So D is not possible.

11 Yitong argues that the government should give a subsidy so that left-handed people can buy left-handed scissors. The statement that there may be higher-priority issues that need financial support from the government most weakens this argument because it undermines the claim and makes it less likely to hold up. Subsidies for left-handed scissors may not be a government priority.

B is incorrect. This statement could strengthen a general argument in favour of having left-handed scissors available for left-handed people to use so they can work faster. However, it neither strengthens nor weakens Yitong's argument that there should be a government subsidy to purchase the scissors.

C is incorrect. This statement does not weaken Yitong's argument; it strengthens it.

D is incorrect. Yitong has already mentioned that the right-handed scissors have caused her pain and uses it as evidence to support her argument.

12 If whoever was selected as player of the match must have had a big impact on the game and must have shown a positive attitude, then it follows that anyone who does not satisfy both requirements cannot have been selected as player of the match. So if Dora did not have a big impact on the game, she cannot have been selected as player of the match.

B is incorrect. Just because Hebe satisfies both requirements, it does not mean she must have been selected as player of the match. There might also be others who satisfy both requirements. It only means that Hebe might have been selected.

C is incorrect. Just because Adam did not have a big impact on the game, it does not mean he did not show a positive attitude.

D is incorrect. Just because Ezra was not selected as player of the match, it does not mean he must not have shown a positive attitude.

13 There are four cards with two sides. So there are eight letters in all: A, B, E, K, N, P, S and T. If two letters are on the same card, they cannot both appear in the same word.

The letter E cannot be on the same card as the A, B, K, P, S or T as it appears in the words STEP, BAKE and BEST alongside them. So the E and the N must be on the same card. This means they cannot appear in a word together.

The letter T cannot be on the same card as the A, B, E, N, P or S as it appears in the words STEP, PANT and BEST alongside them. So the T and the K must be on the same card. This means they cannot appear in a word together.

For similar reasons P and B must be on two sides of the same card, and S and A are on the same card.

Option B (PAST) cannot be spelt out. The S and the A cannot appear in the same word as they are on opposites sides of the same card.

All other options are possible.

14 The purple circle is attached to the left side of purple arrow if the arrow is pointing up. This is not the case in B.

15 If fear of being caught and lunchtime detention is the reason why students don't litter, and therefore the reason the litter guards never catch anyone littering, then being a litter guard might not be a waste of time. So Mr White cannot say it proves being a litter guard is a waste of time and this shows the mistake he has made.

A is incorrect. The information tells us the playground has been litter free for the last two terms so this statement is not correct. However, it is not a mistake made by Mr White.

B is incorrect. This statement could be true so it is not a mistake Mr White has made.

D is incorrect. Just because teachers already have some time to prepare lessons, it does not mean they don't need more time or that there is nothing else more useful they could do with the time. So this is not a mistake Mr White has made.

16 For the conclusion to hold, it must be assumed that not looking at screens so often is a good thing: If you have a pet fish, you won't want to look at a screen so often + not looking at screens so often is a good thing means therefore people should buy a pet fish.

A is incorrect. This does not link the evidence to the conclusion so it is not the assumption made: If you have a pet fish, you won't want to look at a screen so often + there is a new pet store at the shopping centre **does not** mean people should buy a pet fish.

B is incorrect. This is the conclusion, not the missing assumption.

D is incorrect. This is the evidence given to draw the conclusion.

17 You can see from the second statement that the person who has the third-best report also has the most interesting experiment. You need to find out who this is.

The third statement tells you Scarlett's experiment is more interesting than Aiden's and Daphne's. In the question you find out that Aiden's experiment is the second most interesting. This means Scarlett's is the most interesting. This means she has the third-best report.

18 This statement best expresses the main idea. The rest of the text supports this main idea by giving more information and ideas about what you can do at home to help.

A is incorrect. This background information is used in the introduction but it is not the main idea. The main idea is about what you can do at home to help.

B is incorrect. This information is not in the text so it cannot be the main idea.

D is incorrect. This information is not the main idea; it supports the main idea.

19 A 1-m² garden bed needs four 1-m sides as the perimeter is 4 m.

A square 4-m² garden bed needs eight 1-m sides as the perimeter is 8 m. Rectangular garden beds could also have an area of 4 m² but would have a longer perimeter and so would require more kits.

 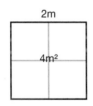

So only two kits in total are needed

20 The information provided gives us at least two people who are learning Mandarin and tells us that the same number of people are learning French as Mandarin. So there must be at least two people learning French but they cannot be either A or B, as these two are learning other languages.

That means at least two of C, D and E must be learning French. However, C lives in Australia and no-one in Australia is learning French so D and E must be the only two students learning French. The answer is D.

All the other options are possible but it isn't clear that they must be true.

SAMPLE TEST 3B Page 57

1 C 2 B 3 A 4 C 5 D 6 B 7 A 8 A 9 D
10 C 11 B 12 D 13 C 14 D 15 D 16 B
17 A 18 D 19 C 20 C

1 Julian finished three places ahead of Aria, which means Julian must have finished in first or second (and Aria must have finished in fourth or fifth). However, Sonny came fourth so Aria must have come fifth. This means Julian must have come second.

Tom beat Lim so Tom came first and Lim came third.

The final order is: Tom, Julian, Lim, Sonny and then Aria.

2 Looking at the solid in B, you can picture the smaller piece that fits together with it.

 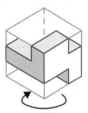

When rotated, this piece is the same as the solid in the question.

3 Only Ruby's reasoning is correct. Since her father always brushes away the spider webs, there might not be many spiders at Ruby's house. And since there are fewer spiders to eat the flies, there could be more flies. However, there is not enough information to say this is definitely the case. So Ruby's reasoning is correct when she says maybe that is why they have a fly problem.

B is incorrect. Alex's reasoning has a flaw because he says it must be the reason why they have a fly problem. There could be other reasons why there are more flies.

C and D are incorrect by a process of elimination.

4 The argument in the question makes a claim and then gives two reasons to support it. Option C makes a claim and then gives two reasons to support it.

A is incorrect. This argument is about the same topic as the one in the box but it doesn't use the same structure. It begins with a claim then gives one reason to support it and ends with a call to action.

B is incorrect. This argument begins by providing evidence and then concludes with the claim.

D is incorrect. This argument makes a claim and then gives three reasons to support it.

5   The order in which the squares should be placed is shown below, together with the pile after each square is added.

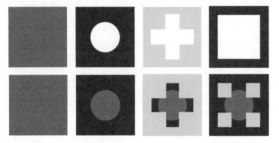

6   Kaylee's conclusion is that there is nothing wrong with going to a beach party at night. She has based this conclusion on the evidence that all her friends are going. So for her conclusion to hold, it must be assumed that it is okay to do something if all your friends are doing it: All my friends are going to the night-time beach party + it's okay to do something if all your friends are doing it means therefore there's nothing wrong with going to a beach party at night.

A is incorrect. This is Kaylee's conclusion, not her assumption.

C is incorrect. This is the evidence Kaylee has used to base her conclusion on.

D is incorrect. This assumption **does not** support Kaylee's conclusion: All my friends are going to the night-time beach party + Kaylee is not allowed to go to the beach at night does not mean therefore there's nothing wrong with going to a beach party at night.

7   As there are three times as many 8-biscuit bags as 5-biscuit bags, there are three possibilities:

Connie could have 1 bag of 5 and 3 bags of 8 biscuits: $1 \times 5 + 3 \times 8 = 29$ biscuits.

She could have 2 bags of 5 and 6 bags of 8 biscuits: $2 \times 5 + 6 \times 8 = 58$ biscuits..

Or she could have 3 bags of 5 and 9 bags of 8: $3 \times 5 + 9 \times 8 = 87$ biscuits..

However, the remaining biscuits must be a multiple of 3 as they are in bags of 3 biscuits each.

In the first case, $90 - 29 = 61$. Sixty-one cannot be made using bags of 3.

In the second case, $90 - 58 = 32$. Thirty-two also cannot be made using bags of 3.

There must be only one bag of 3 biscuits left.

8   After Jin has completed the flips, he has flipped the first card over three times and the third card over once. Flipping them an odd number of times is the same as if he had flipped both of them over just once. The reverse of the first card can either show the shape or it could be blank.

The second card will have been flipped over twice, which is the same as not flipping it over at all. This means it must show the cross. The answer is therefore A.

9   According to the teacher if a student has not practised for at least 20 minutes at least five times a week, then they do not have a chance of winning a prize. Therefore none of the students who practise for less than 20 minutes five times a week will win a prize. So this statement must be true.

A is incorrect. According to the teacher, practising for 20 minutes five times a week gives a student only a chance of winning a prize. It does not guarantee a prize.

B is incorrect. This is the minimum required to have a chance of winning a prize. It does not guarantee a prize. Students who have practised more than this also have a chance of winning a prize.

C is incorrect. The teacher says students must have practised for at least 20 minutes at least five times a week so if a student has practised for less than 20 minutes, they cannot win a prize according to the teacher—even if they have practised more than five times in the week.

10 This statement most strengthens the argument since an international fund could help finance the international research.

A is incorrect. This statement adds evidence to the need to deal with space junk. However, it does not most strengthen the argument about who should pay to deal with it.

B and D are incorrect. These statements weaken the argument rather than strengthen it.

11 Of the numbers 1 to 8, there are three possible pairs that add up to 8. They are 1 + 7, 2 + 6 and 3 + 5. There are also two possible pairs that add up to 5: 1 + 4 and 2 + 3.

You cannot use 2 and 3 for the card with a sum of 5 because either the 2 or the 3 would be needed for one of the cards with a sum of 8.

This means one card has the 1 and 4 on it, which sum to 5. So there cannot be a card with 1 and 7 on it. So one card has the 2 and 6 on it and one card has the 3 and 5 on it, which sum to 8. The last card has the 7 and 8 on it.

It is only possible to see one side of a card at a time so:

A is incorrect as it includes the 1 and the 4.

C is incorrect as it includes the 3 and the 5.

D is incorrect as it includes the 2 and the 6.

12 We know that to qualify for the robotics team, a student must have attended a weekend introduction to robotics workshop. However, that might not be the only criterion used to select team members. It doesn't mean that anyone who attended a workshop will definitely be chosen for the team. So option D shows the flaw in Ivy's reasoning that Bella will definitely be chosen to be in the team this term. Bella might, in fact, not be chosen.

The other options are incorrect. These may be the case but they do not show a mistake Ivy has made.

13 The purple arrow must point directly to the white circle. This is not the case in A.

The white square must be on the left of the purple arrow if we treat the arrow as pointing upwards. This is not the case in either B or D.

14 You can use a basic table with two columns to help you. We can use a square to represent the person with the best stage presence. The circle represents the person with the best voice.

Presence	Voice
□	○
	□
○	

You know that Garant ranks as neither best nor worst in either category so he cannot be the circle or the square. Garant must finish third in the voice category.

If Ming has the second-best stage presence, she also cannot be the circle or square. She must then have the worst voice.

Presence	Voice
□	○
Ming	□
Garant	Garant
○	Ming

15 It takes Colleen 1 h 15 to travel the loop. It takes Braith 5 hours, which is four times as long.

So Colleen is four times as fast as Braith and that means she travels four times as far in the same time. This means when Braith has travelled one-fifth of the loop, Colleen will have travelled the other four-fifths.

If we divide the time it takes Braith into five equal parts, they will pass each other after one of those parts.

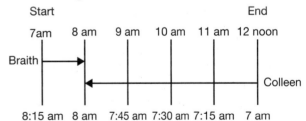

They pass each other at exactly 8 am.

16 From the information given, you can draw the conclusion that if Carlos was tired and looked a mess at the interview, he would not make a good impression. And if he does not make a good impression, he does not stand a chance of getting the job. So this conclusion cannot be true.

A is incorrect. This statement might be true. Even though Carlos went to the movies, he might not have looked a mess and been tired at the interview. The information tells us he will likely look a mess and be tired, not that he definitely will. And if he is not tired and a mess, he might still make a good impression and be offered the job.

C is incorrect. This statement might be true. The information tells us if Carlos makes a good impression, he might be offered the job—not that he will definitely be offered it.

D is incorrect. This statement might be true. Even if he did not go to the movies with Luna, Carlos might still not have made a good impression. Or he might have made a good impression and still not been offered the job for some other reason. The information tells us he might be offered the job if he makes a good impression.

17 Only Livvy's reasoning is correct. Since Emily and Alice were only allowed to go to the party if they had tidied their own bedroom, then if Alice was going to the party she must have tidied her bedroom.

B is incorrect. Dylan's reasoning has a flaw. Just because Emily is not going to the party, it does not follow that she did not tidy her room. It is possible that Emily is not going for some other reason. So Dylan cannot say she must not have tidied her room. He can only say she might not have.

C and D are incorrect by a process of elimination.

18 The owner argues that the new wave pool will benefit the whole town because it will give the young people of the town the opportunity to surf. However, if the club is an exclusive facility for members only, then that opportunity will only be available to club members and not the whole town. So this statement limits the scope of the claim and therefore undermines and weakens it.

A is incorrect. This statement supports the club owner's evidence that people will be able to surf in the pool, even though there is not a beach in site. So it doesn't weaken the owner's argument.

B is incorrect. This statement might support the background technology information given by the owner, but it neither strengthens nor weakens the owner's argument that the new wave pool will benefit the whole town because it will give the young people of the town the opportunity to surf.

C is incorrect. This statement neither strengthens nor weakens the argument about the benefit to the whole town based on the opportunity to surf.

19 For Violet's conclusion to hold, it must be assumed that George and Violet must not encourage Ben to eat junk food: If George and Violet buy hot chips, it will encourage Ben to eat junk food + George and Violet must not encourage Ben to eat junk food means therefore George and Violet must not buy hot chips.

A is incorrect. This doesn't link the evidence to Violet's conclusion so it isn't the assumption she has made: If George and Violet buy hot chips, it will encourage Ben to eat junk food + there is a shop nearby that sells hot chips **does not** mean George and Violet must not buy hot chips.

B is incorrect. This is Violet's conclusion, not the missing assumption.

D is incorrect. This is the evidence Violet has used to draw her conclusion.

20 This is best explained using a table of the five musicians.

The only person who doesn't play the piano has brown eyes. So it cannot be W, as W has blue eyes. This means W plays piano as well as guitar. It is now known what V and W play.

Two of the unmentioned musicians must play the piano and the person who doesn't play has brown eyes. Two people play the saxophone. If they also play the piano, then the brown-eyed person plays the drums and guitar. But this would mean that there were the same number of people who play guitar as play the drums. You are told this is not the case. So the person with brown eyes plays the saxophone and the guitar and the other two people play the instruments shown.

Eye colour		Blue			Brown
	V	W			
Piano	✓	✓	✓	✓	
Drums	✓				
Guitar		✓	✓		✓
Saxophone				✓	✓

T can be any of the unnamed people in the table. No-one plays the same instruments as V. The only person who plays the same instruments as someone else is W. So if T plays the same as someone, it must be W. No other option is possible.

SAMPLE TEST 4A Page 62

> 1 D 2 B 3 A 4 D 5 B 6 C 7 B 8 C 9 B
> 10 D 11 D 12 D 13 A 14 D 15 A 16 A
> 17 B 18 D 19 B 20 B

1 Sandrine completed more questions correctly than Ryder but fewer than Billa. Billa completed fewer than Violet. This means Ryder finished below Violet, Billa and Sandrine. He could have come fourth or fifth. If he came fourth, the only other place left for Lucas is fifth.

2 Since Anh had a record of previous interest in filmmaking, the result of the music test was not relevant in his case. He only had to pass the public-speaking challenge to attend the filming of the program. Since he was not selected to attend, he must have failed the public-speaking challenge.

A is incorrect. This statement might be true. However, since Anh had a record of previous interest in filmmaking, the result of the music test was not relevant in his case. Therefore it cannot be the reason he was not selected.

C is incorrect. The question tells us Anh had a record of previous interest in filmmaking.

D is incorrect. Since Anh had a record of previous interest in filmmaking, he only had to pass the public-speaking challenge to be selected to attend the filming of the program.

So this statement that he did well in the challenge cannot be true since Anh failed to be selected. Since it cannot be true, it cannot be the reason.

3 Only Aida's reasoning is correct. Aida's dog is not a Labrador. However, the information states that Labradors tend to weigh more than other breeds, not that they always weigh more. So Aida is correct when she says her dog might weigh more.

B is incorrect. Jackson's reasoning has a flaw. Just because Labradors tend to weigh more than other breeds, it does not follow that they always weigh more. Thus Jackson cannot say his dog must weigh over 30 kilos. It is also possible that Jackson's dog is not fully grown, since no information is given about its age. In this case, his reasoning would still be flawed.

C and D are incorrect by a process of elimination.

4 Looking at the solid in D, you can picture the smaller piece that fits together with it.

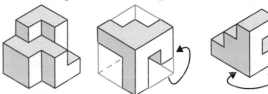

When rotated, this piece is the same as the solid in the question.

5 This statement, that pets can be an exciting distraction, could undermine Felicity's claim that the pets in the classroom will be a positive influence since the distraction could disrupt learning. This would not be a positive influence so this statement most weakens Felicity's argument.

A is incorrect. This statement provides further evidence to support Felicity's claim about the positive influence of pets. Therefore it strengthens the argument rather than weakens it.

C is incorrect. This statement neither strengthens nor weakens Felicity's argument. It is irrelevant to the argument about being allowed to bring pets into the classroom because it will have a positive influence on students.

D is incorrect. This statement provides further evidence to support Felicity's claim about the positive influence of pets so it strengthens the argument rather than weakens it.

6 The order in which the squares should be placed is shown below, together with the pile after each square is added.

7 If Blake has the same number of 10c and 50c coins, these coins have a value that is a multiple of 60c.

If he has one of each coin, he has
$0.10 + $0.50 = $0.60.

If he has two of each coin, he has
2 × $0.10 + 2 × $0.50 = $1.20.

So the value must be either 60c, $1.20, $1.80, etc.

Similarly if he has the same number of 5c and 20c coins, these coins have a value that is a multiple of 25c.

If he has one of each coin, he has
$0.05 + $0.20 = $0.25.

If he has two of each coin, he has
2 × $0.05 + 2 × $0.20 = $0.50.

So the value must be either 25c, 50c, 75c, $1, etc.

A total of $3.75 means that Blake must have an odd number of 5c and 20c coins, as an even number will result in a final digit of 0.

If he has one 5c and one 20c, the other coins must have a value of $3.50. But this is not a multiple of $0.60 so it cannot be the case.

If he has three 5c and three 20c coins, the other coins must have a value of $3.00 which is possible, as this is a multiple of $0.60.

3 × $0.05 + 5 × $0.10 + 3 × $0.20 + 5 × $0.50 = $3.75

There are 16 coins altogether.

8 Daisy assumes that since four local competitions were won by students from her school during the year, there must be four students who won those competitions. However, it may be that some students won more than one competition. In this case fewer than half of the qualifiers could be competition winners. Therefore option C is correct.

The other options are incorrect. These statements could be true but they are irrelevant to Daisy's claim and not mistakes Daisy has made.

9 This statement most strengthens Talia's argument that the nets are not effective: if the sharks are caught on their way out from the beach, the net hasn't stopped them swimming to the beach.

A is incorrect. This statement would strengthen an argument for using other means to protect beachgoers. However, it does not most strengthen Talia's argument that shark nets are not an effective way to protect swimmers.

C is incorrect. This statement is irrelevant to Talia's argument about the effectiveness of the nets.

D is incorrect. This statement contradicts Talia's evidence about the nets being only 150 metres long, so it could undermine her argument and weaken it.

10 The back of the second card must be a shape. It cannot be blank. This rules out A.

The back of the third card is either a cross or is blank. This rules out C.

The back of the fourth card must be a shape. It cannot be blank. This rules out B.

11 The argument in the question makes a claim, gives two reasons to support that claim and ends with a call to action. Option D also makes a claim, gives two reasons to support that claim and ends with a call to action.

A is incorrect. This argument is about the same topic as the one given but it does not follow the same structure. It begins with a claim, then gives only one reason to support that claim and does not end with a call to action.

B is incorrect. This argument begins by providing evidence and then concludes with the claim.

C is incorrect. This argument makes a claim and then gives two reasons to support it but it does not end with a call to action.

12 Statement D best expresses the main idea. It is the main idea Stella wants readers to accept. The rest of the text supports this main idea by giving more information about krill and why it should be protected.

A is incorrect. This information is used in the introduction but it is not the main idea. It supports the main idea.

B is incorrect. This information is not in the text so it cannot be the main idea.

C is incorrect. This information is not the main idea. It supports the main idea.

13 This is easiest to understand if you draw a simple diagram.

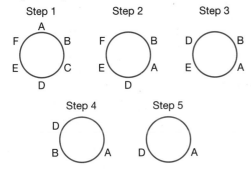

Step 1   Step 2   Step 3

Step 4   Step 5

The starting positions are shown in Step 1. After Ash has had his go, he has taken Candice's spot and there are now five people left. This is shown in Step 2. After Desh's go, Fernand is eliminated (Step 3) and it is now Bongo's turn. Bongo takes Elliot's spot (Step 4) and it is Desh's turn. Desh takes Bongo's spot and only Desh and Ash remain (Step 5).

14 Grace has dinosaurs and unicorns but neither Evie nor Lily has these backpack toys.

A is incorrect. Grace does not have dogs or cartoon-character backpack toys.

B is incorrect. Grace has ponies and dinosaurs but Lily also has ponies.

C is incorrect. Grace has unicorns and sea creatures but both Evie and Lily also have sea creatures.

15 This outcome is not possible. If Will passed the analysis component, then he must have passed one other component. Will cannot have passed research because everyone who passed research also passed the presentation component. If this were true, it would mean Will had passed all three components but the information tells us no-one passed all three components.

B is incorrect. This outcome could be true. Will could have failed analysis and research but still passed the presentation component.

C is incorrect. This outcome could be true. Just because no-one who passed research failed the presentation component, it does not mean that someone didn't pass the presentation component but failed research.

D is incorrect. This outcome could be true. If Will passed analysis, then he must have passed at least one other component. Will cannot have passed research because everyone who passed research also passed the presentation component. If this were true, it would mean Will had passed all three components. However, the information tells us no-one passed all three components so Will could have passed analysis and the presentation component.

16 In the net, the white square is attached to the right side of the white arrow if the arrow is pointing up. This is not the case in B or in D so we can rule them both out. In the net, the white square is also on the right side of the purple arrow if the arrow is pointing up. This is not the case in C so we can rule it out.

17 You need to find out who made the worst egg cups. This is based on the scores given.

Virginia scored higher than Yang, Winnie scored higher than Zan, and Zan scored higher than Virginia. The order from best to worst is Winnie, Zan, Virginia, Yang.

Yang made the worst egg cups. You now need to find out where Yang ranks in terms of the number of egg cups made.

Virginia made fewer egg cups than Zan, who made fewer than Yang. Yang made fewer egg cups than Winnie. So the order of egg cups made from most to fewest is Winnie, Yang, Zan, Virginia.

Yang made the second-most egg cups.

18 Neither Carlos's nor Ashlee's reasoning is correct.

Carlos says Kyle will be a successful beekeeper for sure and Kyle appears to have the qualities needed. However, the information does not say that someone with those qualities will definitely be a successful beekeeper. Carlos's reasoning is therefore flawed.

Ashlee's reasoning is also flawed. She tells us that Loren has many of the qualities needed to be a beekeeper except that Ashlee thinks Loren is scared of bees. Since Ashlee does not know for sure that Loren is scared of bees, she cannot say being a beekeeper is definitely not for Loren.

19 The first rectangle can be broken into three sections with dimensions 4 m by 3 m. Each of these smaller rectangles will take 15 minutes to tile. Two of these sections will fit perfectly into the second rectangle. So it will take two lots of 15 minutes. The answer is B: 30 minutes.

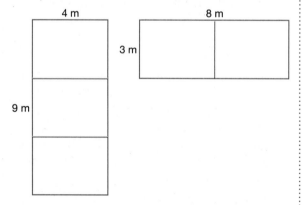

20 In D the bakery is two storeys high when it is only meant to be one storey. So you can rule out D.

In A the music store is not directly to the left of the hardware store so you can rule out A.

In C the bakery and music store are separated by only one store, not two, as is meant to be the case. You can rule out C.

The answer is B.

SAMPLE TEST 4B

Page 67

1 A 2 D 3 D 4 C 5 C 6 B 7 B 8 A 9 B
10 C 11 A 12 C 13 C 14 B 15 D 16 C
17 A 18 B 19 C 20 A

1 Cai beat Bodhi but finished after Inara. This means Cai cannot finish first or fifth. If Elio finishes two ahead of Cai, Cai cannot finish second.

Cai could finish in third or fourth place. Elio must finish two places ahead of Cai. Inara must also finish ahead of Cai, and Bodhi must finish after her. The four possible orders are shown below:

Place				
1	Elio	Elio	Freya	Inara
2	Inara	Inara	Elio	Elio
3	Cai	Cai	Inara	Freya
4	Bodhi	Freya	Cai	Cai
5	Freya	Bodhi	Bodhi	Bodhi

Freya can finish in any place except second.

2 Looking at the solid in D, you can picture the smaller piece that fits together with it.

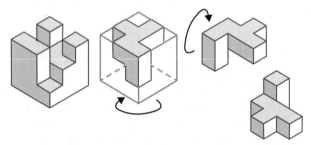

When rotated, this piece is the same as the solid in the question.

3 This statement strengthens the principal's argument by providing further evidence that recess is good for student wellbeing.

A is incorrect. This is the principal's argument so simply restating it does not strengthen it.

B is incorrect. This statement is irrelevant to the principal's argument about student health and wellbeing. In fact, it could weaken a general argument to increase recess time.

C is incorrect. This statement is irrelevant to the principal's argument about increased recess time being good for student health and wellbeing.

4   The argument in the box makes a claim and then gives one reason to support it. Option C also makes a claim and then gives one reason to support it.

A is incorrect. This argument begins by providing two reasons to support a claim and then concludes with the claim.

B is incorrect. This argument begins with a claim and gives one reason in support but ends with a call to action.

D is incorrect. This argument makes a claim and then gives two reasons to support it.

5   The motel has the same number of triple rooms as family rooms. If there is one triple and one family room, they sleep 8 people ($5 + 3 = 8$). If there are two triples and two family rooms, they sleep 16 people ($2 \times 3 + 2 \times 5 = 16$). So the triple and family rooms must sleep 8, 16, 24 or 32 people.

Looking at the options:

Option A will sleep 4 people in 2 double rooms (as there are 2 people per room), meaning there are 32 people sleeping in 4 triple rooms and 4 family rooms. This is the correct number of people but the wrong number of rooms. There are only 10 rooms. **Option A is incorrect.**

Option B and Option D are also incorrect. It is not possible to sleep exactly 36 people if there are 4 or 8 double rooms.

Option C is correct. Six double rooms and three each of the triple and family rooms will give 36 people in 12 rooms.

6   The order in which the squares should be placed is shown below, together with the pile after each square is added.

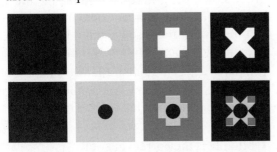

7   Statement B cannot be true. Sara finished second but was slower than Terry so Terry must have been first to finish the course.

A is incorrect. This statement could be true.

C is incorrect. This statement is true.

D is incorrect. We don't know whether this statement is true or not, since we don't know how many mistakes Kimberley made. Therefore it is not possible to state that it cannot be true.

Name	Fastest time	Mistakes made
Terry	1st	3
Sara	2nd	2
Monti	3rd or 4th	1 or none
Kimberley	3rd or 4th	Not known
Anjar	5th	none

8   Statement A, that military spending can create jobs, limits the scope of the claim that money would be better spent on unemployment programs. So this statement most weakens the argument.

B is incorrect. This statement could weaken an argument against military spending but it doesn't most weaken the argument about the money being better spent on social or humanitarian issues.

C and D are incorrect. These statements do not weaken the argument.

9   Rohan says he will win a prize for sure whereas his teacher says completing the challenge and showcasing at least three skills gives only a chance of winning a prize.

A is incorrect. This statement is irrelevant to winning a prize and is not a mistake Rohan made has made.

C is incorrect. This statement does not show a mistake Rohan has made.

D is incorrect. This statement does not show a mistake Rohan has made. There is nothing about a time limit in the information given by the teacher, plus these students may not have showcased enough skills.

10   There are four combinations that sum to 10. They are $9 + 1$, $8 + 2$, $7 + 3$ and $6 + 4$. Two of these must be used.

There are three combinations that sum to 14. They are $10 + 4$, $9 + 5$ and $8 + 6$. One of these combinations is not used on a card. If 10 and 4 are not on the same card, the other combinations are.

However, this would mean that no two cards could both sum to 10. If 9 and 5, as well as 8 and 6, are used to make two cards of 14, only one of the combinations that make 10 is possible $(7 + 3)$. So it must be true that 10 and 4 are on the same card.

11 The main idea the creator of the text wants you to accept is that a new Farmers' Market will be trialled next Saturday at Waratah Park. The rest of the text gives more information about the market to support that main idea.

B and D are incorrect. These statements from the text provide supporting information for the main idea.

C is incorrect. This information is not in the text so cannot be the main idea.

12 In the net, the purple arrow is connected to and pointing to the white square. This is not the case in option A so we can rule it out. In the net, the white arrow is connected to, and pointing at, the purple circle. This is not the case in D so we can rule it out. Option B is incorrect as the circle and purple square shown would be swapped if the white square was shown on top of the dice.

13 The information given doesn't mention Nathan and assists in the same statement. So you will have to use the other information to work it out.

You can use a basic table with two columns to help you. You cannot know who the person with the most assists is but can use a shape to represent them. Here we have used a square.

The person with the fewest assists is represented by the circle.

Assists	Points	
☐		1st
	◯	↑
◯	☐	4th

You are told that Zoe ranks second for assists, which means she is not the square or the circle. You are also told that Nathan scores more points than Zoe. For this to be possible Zoe cannot score the most points. She must also rank second for points.

Nathan therefore also cannot be the square or the circle.

Assists	Points	
☐	Nathan	1st
Zoe	Zoe	↑
Nathan	◯	↓
◯	☐	4th

So he must come third for assists.

14 It takes Pamela 1 hour to paint a rectangle that is 4 m by 2.5 m. So it will take her 30 minutes to paint a rectangle half that size, or 2 m by 2.5 m.

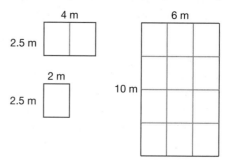

A room of 6 m by 10 m is exactly 12 times as big as the 2 m by 2.5 m rectangle, or six times bigger than the original room. It will take exactly six times as long to paint as the first room. Pamela will finish painting it 6 hours after 9 am, at 3 pm.

15 **Option A is incorrect** as the computer room is not connected directly with the kitchen.

By counting the grid squares in the picture you can see that the L-shaped room in the corner is not the largest room so it cannot be the presentation room. **Option B is incorrect.**

Similarly you can see that the two smallest rooms are not the same size so they cannot be the kitchen and meeting room. **Option C is incorrect.**

Option D is the correct answer.

16 Both Locky and Remie use correct reasoning.

Locky correctly reasons that if the scores in one area were different but the scores in the other area were the same, then their results could not have been equal.

Remie correctly reasons that if the scores in one area were the same but the scores in the other area were different, then their overall scores could not have been equal.

The other options are incorrect by a process of elimination.

17 Ms Wilson's conclusion is that the dog park near the little penguin nesting sites should not be closed. She has based this conclusion on her evidence that if the dog park is closed, it will impact all dog owners in the area. So for her conclusion to hold it must be assumed we should not do something that will impact dog owners in the area: If the dog park is closed, it will impact all dog owners in the area + we should not do something that will impact dog owners in the area means therefore the dog park near the little penguin nesting sites should not be closed.

B is incorrect. This is Ms Wilson's conclusion.

C is incorrect. This is the evidence Ms Wilson gave to draw her conclusion.

D is incorrect. You might assume this is the real reason why Ms Wilson does not want the dog park to close. However, it does not link the evidence to Ms Wilson's conclusion so it is not the assumption she has made based on that evidence.

18 If Pippa is lying, then Daniel didn't do it. In which case Daniel is telling the truth. Since we are told that only one student is telling the truth, the second student who is lying must be Harry. Therefore Harry must also have been the student who drew on the whiteboard.

A is incorrect. If Daniel is lying, then it must have been Daniel who drew on the whiteboard. In this case both Harry and Pippa are telling the truth. However, we are told that only one student is telling the truth so this option cannot be correct.

C is incorrect. If Harry did not draw on the whiteboard, then Harry is telling the truth. Since we know only one student is telling the truth, the other two must therefore be lying. However, it is impossible for both Daniel and Pippa to be lying so this option must be incorrect.

D is incorrect. If Pippa drew on the whiteboard, then Pippa is lying. And if Pippa did it, then both Harry and Daniel are telling the truth. However, we know that only one student is telling the truth so this option is impossible and therefore incorrect.

19 C is the only option that is **not** possible.

The other options are incorrect by a process of elimination. They are all possible.

20 It is important to note there are no references to direction in this question; that is, no box is to the RIGHT or the LEFT of another. This means the order of the boxes can be reflected and we will still get the same answer.

If the red box and the green box are separated by two other boxes, one of them must be at the end of the row, as there are only five boxes. We find out that the red box is not at the end of the row so the green box must be. The white box is at the other end. The black box is next to the green so the yellow must be the middle box.

The board game is in a box at the end of the row but the green box is empty. So it must be in the white box and the necklace must be in the red box next to it. Brenda will find the necklace in the red box.

White	Red	Yellow	Black	Green
Board game	Necklace		Camera	

NOTES

NOTES

NOTES